CREDO

Meditations on the Nicene Creed

SECOND EDITION

DONALD T. WILLIAMS

STONE TOWER PRESS

Original edition published by Chalice Press, 2007.

Stone Tower Press
7 Ellen Rd.
Middletown, RI 02842
stonetowerpress.com

ISBN: 979-8-9992313-2-1

Formatting and cover design by Amy Cole, JPL Design Solutions

Printed in the United States of America

For

MICHAEL BAUMAN

Fellow Lover of

Erasmus and Milton,

Good Letters,

Christian Truth,

Christ.

TABLE OF CONTENTS

ACKNOWLEDGMENTS

Some of my debts are acknowledged in the Introduction. The Nicene Fathers were of course indispensable, but Franz Schubert and Robert Shaw also made contributions to this project of which they had no knowledge and for which they bear no responsibility. They have my gratitude nonetheless.

In addition, portions of the manuscript while it was in preparation have been read by such friends and scholars as Michael Bauman, Ruby Dunlap, Mark and Debby Gerl, Brian and Kami Melton, Jaime Fredericks McCall, Matt Preston, Ken and Cindy Morefield, and Todd and Sherry Truffin, several of whom were members of Inklings II (Inklings Too, Inklings To...), the writers and artists support group of Trinity Fellowship Evangelical Free Church of Toccoa, GA. Their suggestions and encouragement have been invaluable. My own poems which appear are from *Stars through the Clouds: The Collected Poetry of Donald T. Williams* (Lynchburg: Lantern Hollow Press, 2020) and used by permission.

The idea for the Prayers after each meditation came from a friend who wrote a good many for her own devotional purposes as she read the manuscript. They became the basis for the ones which appear in the book. May they help lead us back to the Lord whose praise is our highest reason for being.

PRELUDE

CREDO
VILLANELLE NO. 25

The content, the commitment we express
When mind and heart embrace the ancient Creed
Are faith and fealty. That we confess
Our faith means it is more than just a guess:
Our Lord's own blood is what has guaranteed
The content, so commitment we express.
Acknowledging the Law that we transgress,
We find forgiveness, know that we are freed
To faith and fealty when we confess.
We walk by faith, not sight. Still, nonetheless,
We've tasted and we've seen, and so we feed.
The content's the commitment we express.
This ceremonial assent, this "Yes!"
Flows gladly from both mind and heart: the deed
Is faith and fealty when we confess.
Not just a ritual; it is more, not less:
We stake our very souls, for when we plead
This content, the commitment we express
Is faith and fealty when we confess.

–D.T.W.

CREDO:
MEDITATIONS ON THE NICENE CREED

INTRODUCTION

You hold in your hands an anomaly. What is it? A devotional book with substantive theological content? A book of serious theology with a devotional bent? Can there even be such a thing? Yes. As such, it is an attempt to heal, to bind together, the gaping wounds that Theology and Devotion have both received from living in our intellectually fragmented age.

The most important words in this book are not mine. That is, I did not compose them, though I have adopted them and embraced them as being the most important and authoritative words ever written outside of Scripture itself. They were set down at Nicaea in A.D. 325, expanded at Constantinople in 381, and confirmed at Chalcedon in 451, as the Church met in search of formulae which could preserve the Gospel of the salvation God had wrought in Jesus Christ from dilution by paganism and rationalism.

ON TO NICAEA

"*...fides quaerens intellectum*"—Anselm of Canterbury

From the first day the Gospel was proclaimed
The passionate intellect was there, demanding,
Not proof—the Empty Tomb provided that—
But reasoned explanation that was aimed
At Faith in search of fruitful understanding
For mindful worship, not for idle chat.

So the Apostles, sent to meet this need,
Defined with care the doctrine they were handing
To their disciples; they to those who sat
At their feet. Faithfully they sowed the Seed,
Watered, weeded, wept through heat and cold
(Scripture was the standard, guaranteed,
By which they worked as on the seasons rolled)
Until it brought forth light a hundredfold,
A wholesome harvest on which yet we feed.
The climax of this process was the Creed.

(D.T.W.)

For more than a millennium and a half now those words have served that purpose well, and continue to do so for orthodox Christians of all communions. They appear here, phrase by phrase and sometimes even word by word, as chapter headings or, perhaps more accurately, as the wellsprings or fountainheads of the meditations to which they have given rise. That they do so is proof that they continue to achieve their ancient purpose in me; my hope is that they will do so in you as well.

The other words had their origins, one might say, in 1815 when Franz Schubert decided to score the accompaniment for his *Mass in G* for strings and organ only, leaving out the wind parts. That decision produced something of a dilemma for the second clarinetist in the orchestra at Georgia's Governor's Honors Program (an advanced summer institute for gifted high school students) in 1968. Robert Shaw, freshly hired as music director for the Atlanta Symphony, was coming to conduct Schubert's *Mass* with combined orchestra and chorus, and the chance to work with Shaw was not to be missed. So despite the fact that the student was a much better clarinetist than a vocalist, he wrangled permission to transfer to the chorus for the occasion.

It was a heady experience for the young fundamentalist to encounter the Creed for the first time in its ancient Latin text, in the supremely appropriate musical setting of Schubert (the hushed contemplation of the Trinitarian ontology, the strident anger of the *Crucifixus*, the ethereal rapture of the *Et Resurrexit*), under the incomparable direction of Shaw. He noted with pleasure that his foreign-language skills, though then mostly based on Latin's younger daughter Spanish, enabled him to translate much of it at sight and eventually to figure out the rest. He noted with surprise his ability to affirm every word of what he then considered a Roman Catholic creed, and with interest its omission of the crucial insights of the Reformation: *Sola Scriptura, Sola Gratia, Sola Fide,* Scripture alone, Grace alone, Faith alone. He thereby learned a great deal about the real nature of his differences with the church of Rome. He noted with admiration the simplicity and beauty as well as the truth of the text and thus developed a life-long love affair with those elegant, direct, and expressive summations of his own deepest commitments in their ancient form. He has come back to them time and time again in the ensuing years, and the meditations in this book are the result.

He remains deeply committed to the theology of the Reformation, holding it to be the most consistent development of the even more basic insights delineated by the ancient Church. (See his book *Ninety-Five Theses for a New Reformation: A Road Map for Post-Evangelical Christianity, Semper Reformanda* Publications, 2021). Calvin, for example, organized his great theological masterpiece, *The Institutes of the Christian Religion,* on a pattern borrowed from the Creeds, with sections on the Father, the Son, the Spirit, and the Church. Thus, like the Reformers, the author affirms the value of the Creed precisely because he is committed to Scripture as the only final authority. Both the Creed and the Church derive their authority from their relation to Scripture; The Creed is authoritative because the Church has universally recognized it as an accurate summary of many of the most basic teachings of the Bible. Unlike Scripture, it is not necessarily infallible; but because it is a summary of Scripture and a focusing of Scripture in the light of crucial questions which continue to be relevant, it is profound and it is useful. As the man the student of 1968 grew into, I commend it to you as such, hoping you will find it as inspiring as I have found it.

In expounding the Creed, I have tried to follow two principles which may not always seem entirely compatible. First, I have tried to elucidate the unified core of Christian truth it contains which transcends the denominational distinctives that have developed over the years, believing that this core of truth is valuable as the proper basis of Christian unity.

But second, in doing this I have made no attempt to disguise the perspective from which I view these affirmations: that of conservative Protestant Evangelicalism. There is sometimes a certain tension between these two goals, with the exposition sometimes veering more toward the ecumenical, sometimes the Evangelical pole. But there is a method to my madness. I have found working within that tension a useful and profitable exercise. And thus I hope my Evangelical cohorts will come to see the Creed as both an expression of their own faith and a bridge to those in other historic Christian communities who have not yet bowed the knee to the false gods of liberalism and secular thought. And I hope that my Roman Catholic and Orthodox friends may also find something of value here, and find that the traffic on that bridge can move both ways.

Soli Deo gloria!

Donald T. Williams
Toccoa Falls, Ga.

THE NICENE CREED

Credo in unum Deum,	I believe in one God,
Patrem omnipotentem,	the Father Almighty,
factorem coeli et terrae,	maker of heaven and earth,
visibilium omnium et invisibilium,	and of all things visible and invisible,
et in unum Dominum, Jesum Christum,	and in one Lord, Jesus Christ,
Filium Dei unigenitum,	the only-begotten Son of God,
ex Patre natum, ante omnia saecula,	born of the Father before all ages,
Deum de Deo, lumen de lumine,	God of God, light of light,
Deum verum de Deo vero,	very God of very God,
genitum non factum,	begotten, not made,
con substantialem Patri,	of one substance with the Father
per quem omnia facta sunt,	by whom all things were made,
qui propter nos homines	who for us men
et propter nostram salutem	and for our salvation
descendit de coelis. Et incarnatus	came down from heaven. And became incarnate

est de Spiritu sancto ex Maria	by the Holy Ghost of the Virgin Mary
Virgine et homo factus est,	and was made man,
crucifixus etiam pro nobis	and was crucified also for us
sub Pontio Pilato,	under Pontius Pilate,
passus et sepultus est,	suffered and was buried,
Et resurrexit tertia die	and the third day He rose again
secundum scripturas,	according to the Scriptures,
et ascendit in coelum,	and ascended into heaven,
sedet ad dexteram Patris,	and sitteth on the right hand of the Father,
et iterum venturus est cum gloria	and He shall come again with glory
judicare vivos et mortuos,	to judge the living and the dead,
cuius regni non erit finis.	whose kingdom shall have no end.
Et in Spiritum Sanctum,	And in the Holy ghost,
Dominum et vivificantem,	the lord and life-giver,
qui ex Patre Filioque procedit,	who proceedeth from the Father and the Son,
qui cum Patre et Filio	who with the Father and the Son
simul adoratur et conglorificatur,	together is adored and glorified,
qui locutus est per prophetas,	who spake by the prophets,

et unum sanctum catholicam	and in one holy catholic
et apostolicam ecclesiam,	and apostolic Church,
confiteor unum baptisma	I acknowledge one baptism
in remissionem peccatorum,	for the remission of sins,
et expecto resurrectionem	and I expect the resurrection
mortuorum,	of the dead,
et vitam venturi saeculi,	and the life of the world to come,
Amen.	Amen.

II

THE FATHER

Credo
"I Believe..."

Christians by definition *believe* in one God, the Father almighty, maker of heaven and earth. They believe in one Lord, Jesus Christ, the only begotten Son of the Father, who for us men and for our salvation descended from Heaven and was incarnate by the Holy Spirit in the Virgin Mary and was made man—who in pursuit of this mission was crucified under Pontius Pilate, died, and was buried, but rose on the third day and ascended into heaven, whence he will return at the end of the age to judge the quick and the dead. They believe in the Holy Spirit and in one holy, universal, and apostolic Church, and they believe in the resurrection of the dead and the unending life of glory to follow for all believers. They accept the words of Jesus that whoever *believes* in Him will not perish but enjoy that eternal life (Jn. 3:16) and the teaching of Paul that justification, the declaration of acquittal from sin which serves as their ticket for admission to that life, comes by faith—that is, in Greek the same noun we also translate as *belief*—alone (Rom. 3:26, 28, 10:9–10, Eph. 2:8–10, etc.). All this makes belief and believing very much a matter of life and death for them and—if they are right—for everyone.

But what does it mean to *believe*? What does a person signify when he says that he believes? Sometimes he expresses *intention*, as when he says, "I believe I will go fishing today." Sometimes it is mere *opinion*, though perhaps based on a measure of fact: "I believe Herschel Walker was the greatest running back in the history of college football." Sometimes he uses it for *knowledge*, especially when what he knows seems contrary to naive experience: "I believe the earth is round, though it sure looks flat from here." He may use the word to express *confidence*, as in "I believe I can do that." Sometimes it conveys mere *hope* or even *wishful thinking*: "I believe the Falcons will win their division this year." It may be used for *preference* or *commitment*

("I believe in free enterprise") or personal *trust* and *loyalty* ("I believe in you"). So what does it mean when we use the noun-agent form as a synonym for a Christian and call him a "*Believer*?"

It is clear that the "belief" in Jesus which makes a person a Christian is not the belief of opinion or even knowledge, for even the devils "believe and tremble" (James 2:19), and their apprehension of the truth does not confer eternal life on them; on the contrary, it adds to their condemnation. They believe, they acknowledge the doctrines as true, but they do not accept or embrace, but rather resist and oppose. They hate the truth (which they cannot help but believe) because it is contrary to them and to everything they have chosen to live for. They therefore illustrate the fact that, while being a Christian necessarily does involve thinking that a substantial number of quite specific propositions are so, mental agreement with those propositions does not in and of itself constitute saving faith.

What does?

The Bible in speaking of Christian belief uses a curious combination of the phrases belief *in* or *on* and belief *that*. Whosoever believes "*in* Him" will not perish but have eternal life (Jn. 3:16); Paul tells the Philippian jailer to believe *on* the Lord Jesus Christ in order to be saved (Acts 16:31). This sounds like the language of *trust* or *personal loyalty*. But Paul tells the Romans that if they confess Jesus as Lord and believe (in their hearts) *that* God raised Him from the dead, they will be saved. This sounds like *knowledge* or opinion; but if belief here is parallel to *confession* of Christ's lordship, as seems likely, then we are also hearing the language of *commitment*.

The Christian then does not simply think that certain ideas are true; he is also *committed* to them in the sense that he bases his life on them and risks his eternal soul on their being so. The one who believes in Jesus for salvation *trusts* Him and is *loyal* to Him as servant to Lord on the basis of his commitment to those truths. Faith is more than mental assent, though it is not less. It is the trust which commits, and to believe is to make an irrevocable decision whereby we enter into a relationship of commitment to the living Savior to become his vassal and take Him as our liege lord and king.

It is a solemn thing to recite the creed: *Credo in unum Deum, Pater omnipotentem...et in unum Dominum, Iesum Christum*. To do so unthinkingly is a kind of blasphemy. To do so like the devils—as a mere expression of our ideas, a list of blocks we might check on an opinion poll, but not as living truths we would stake our eternity on and would die for—is a kind of perjury, a false confession. To do so as an affirmation of our profoundest commitment to the truths we live by and as a way of flying the banner of our deepest allegiance is to understand and recapitulate the biblical pattern, to be partakers of eternal life.

PRAYER: Father, I believe. But neither "I" nor "believe" has meaning apart from Thee. Thou takest what I think to be "I" and showest me my true self hidden in Thee. And what I call "believe" is what Thou suppliest to enable a fitting response to Thee. Help me to yield the self and the belief, both from Thee, back to Thee. Amen.

Credo in unum Deum
"I Believe in One God"

Whatever it is that rules a person's life—whatever it is which he values above all else—whatever constitutes that standpoint from which reality is defined for him, which makes sense of everything else, and by which all else is judged and evaluated—whatever that thing is to which, if necessary, he would sacrifice everything else that he is or has—that is his god. And men are so constituted that, whether or not they admit it, and whether or not they desire it, *something* will play that role in their lives. As certain as the seasons, as inevitable as the tide, the religious character of the species inexorably asserts itself. We *will* worship something; the only question is what?

Living in a secular age grants no exemption from the rule. It only means we have a more pronounced tendency to seek our ultimate integration point in the temporal rather than the eternal. For one man it may be a woman (or for a woman it may be a man). For another it may be a career, for another wealth or prestige or power. For the Hedonist it is pleasure, for the Utilitarian, success; for the more high-minded, other philosophies may come into play. For the atheist, even atheism may be his god. For the most impoverished of all, it may simply be his own ego. But *natura vacuum abhorret,* Nature abhors a vacuum, and human nature is no exception. In no case will the void be left unfilled.

Whether anything which is merely temporal *can* ultimately fill the grand Emptiness around which our lives are organized is a question worth asking. Historically, in periods when the gods are finite, a multiplicity of gods have clamored for our allegiance. To attempt to worship more than one is to divide one's very soul in twain; hence, while we may recognize the claims of many and hesitate long between two opinions, there is only one at a time which can really rule our destinies, even if the confusion of pantheism keeps us from recognizing which it is. For the full integration of the personality demands that there be only one Center. That is why the ancient Hindus recognized the principle of the *ishta devata*: you may acknowledge a whole pantheon of deities, but only one will be *your God*. Until you find him you will be a double-minded man, unstable in all your ways. And as long as the god you serve is anything that is temporal and finite, it will always face competition from a host of other potential claimants. Thus a secular age always of necessity fosters spiritual schizophrenia at worst and an unrooted, desperate restlessness at best. Augustine was right: the vacuum in our hearts *is* Trinity shaped, and nothing less than the one infinite and personal Triune God can ultimately fill it. We are restless indeed until we rest in Him.

As the recipients of special revelation, the ancient Hebrews were the first to grasp both the unity and the identity of the One for whom we were made. Thus they grounded their whole theology on the *shema'*: "Hear O Israel, the Lord your God, the Lord is one" (Deut. 6:4). The Hebrew can perhaps more accurately be translated, "Hear O Israel, *Yahweh* is your God, Yahweh *alone*." And they grounded their whole ethic on the command to have no other gods before Him, to love Him with all their heart, soul, mind, and strength, and to serve Him only. They had a precise technical term for the willingness to settle for anything less: *idolatry*. By insisting that all of life be grounded in Yahweh Alone, they affirmed both *One* God and One *God*. In this, they were narrow, intolerant, dogmatic—and right. And when we take the Christian credo in our mouths, we stake our claim to the same ground they occupied, at the foot of the burning Mountain in the presence of the living God.

PRAYER: Father, Thou knowest my belief to be as feeble and as fragmented as my conception of Thee. Grant that my life may increasingly reflect the unity Thou art in Thyself, the one, true God revealed in Jesus Christ Whom Thou hast sent. Amen.

Patrem
"I Believe in One God, the *Father* Almighty"

It was Jesus Himself who taught us to think of God as our Father in heaven. The paternal metaphor was not original with Him, but no one else had ever used it so pervasively, so confidently, and so intimately. No wonder: He was, after all, the Son who had from eternity come from the bosom of the Father. As Jesus was the uniquely begotten (*monogenes, unigenitum*) Son, so God was the uniquely and supremely begetting Father. And so profoundly intertwined is their relationship in the heart of God's Trinitarian Being that neither can be understood except in relation to the other. To really understand Jesus is to worship Him as the Son of God; to really understand God is to know Him as the Father who is worthy of such a Son.

Deeply ingrained in the heart of every son is an unending, compelling desire and drive to please his father, to make his father proud of him. As I first wrote these words, I was conscious of an ongoing silent prayer, almost desperate in intensity, that my father, who was eighty-plus at the time of writing, might live to see them published. (He did.) It mattered—beyond all reason it mattered—simply because I was his son. And I at fifty was no different from my own boy at seventeen, though he was going through the stage of life when he might for a time have found those filial instincts hard to admit to. But they will rule his life in a great way nonetheless, and few things will do more than the precise nature and quality of our relationship to determine his destiny, for good or ill. Hence nothing has more power than that relationship to drive me to my knees before the only Father who is adequate for such things. This, if nothing else, teaches me my absolute dependence on God's grace.

In this, as in all things (sin excepted), Jesus was one of us, differing only in the degree and the perfection of his devotion. His meat and drink was to do the will of the Father (Jn. 4:34); He did only what He saw the Father doing (Jn. 5:19); and he prepared himself for his death by praying, "Father, the hour is come; glorify the Son, that the Son may glorify thee" (Jn. 17:1). His devotion to the Father and to the Father's cause of a redemption for mankind which would cast no aspersion on the Father's justice extended all the way to the Cross of Calvary, the most grievous part of which was the experience of being rejected by the Father as the bearer of human sin. It is no wonder then that at every moment of His eternal existence save that one, He has the satisfaction of hearing the Father say, "This is my beloved Son, in whom I am well pleased."

This filial consciousness of the Son is then for me a great mystery which sheds light on the even greater mystery of the nature and character of God. For *my* son is definitely his father's son, serving me with the same mixture of devotion and sinful rebellion which I gave to my father and he to his. And I know myself to be unworthy even of *that* love and emulation. What kind of person would it take to be deserving of even this mixed and sin-tainted love? Ah, that would be a man and a father indeed! But then, what kind of person would it take to inspire and be worthy of the unstained and infinite filial devotion of Jesus? Perhaps one of the most profound statements the Bible makes is to call that Person the God and *Father* of our Lord Jesus Christ (Eph. 1:3). And perhaps the most staggering statement it makes about us is that, by his grace, we too may become his sons and call Him *our* Father.

PRAYER: Father, the Lord Jesus taught me to call Thee so and showed me the dimensions of that relatedness by living and dying it. By naming Himself Brother to me, He named me child to Thee, and so in that naming I approach Thee now. Amen.

Omnipotentem
"One God, the Father *Almighty*"

We believe in a God who is omnipotent, the Father Almighty. If He is the maker of heaven and earth, it must indeed be so. Einstein revealed the universe to us as a space-time continuum in which matter and energy are simply interchangeable manifestations of the same force or substance of which all created things consist; which is to say that matter and energy and everything they form are God's inventions, his creations, and depend for their being on his will. Thus energy itself, power, force as we know it, depends in itself for its existence on Him. How then could any power be exerted than which He would not be greater? Who or what could exert it? To look for such a being would be a hopeless task indeed, rather like trying to find a candle which could shine more brightly than the sun.

The sun is the source of all energy and life on earth. Whether we burn wood or fossil fuels, we are just releasing stored sunlight. Wind and water power exploit cycles set in motion in the atmosphere by the uneven distribution of the sun's rays. Chlorophyl traps those rays and transforms them into energy we can use for fueling our own bodies, whether we take it directly from the plants or indirectly from the animals who eat the plants. Even nuclear energy simply taps into the same processes that fuel the sun itself. And all the teeming life of the planet thrives by catching just a minuscule part of the power which the sun is constantly generating and lavishing on the empty and insatiable sponge of space.

Yet even the sun does not shine with a light she can call her own. She was not always there and cannot account for her own existence; she neither created her own fuel nor wrote the laws of its combustion. Pile sun upon sun and link galaxy to galaxy until no computer can store the numbers, and still the aggregate will be impotent to explain its own being. The nuclear furnaces of a trillion stars were lit by the strong right arm of our Father Almighty, and they continue to burn because they are stoked by the bellows of his breath, his creative Word. What then can thwart his designs or dare to oppose his purposes? Whatever power can accomplish, that He can do, and it is pathetically pointless to think of standing in his way. Is anything too hard for the Lord?

So profoundly inescapable is this truth that it has tempted the hasty to multiply conundrums: i.e., can God make a stone so big He can't lift it? The question is widely supposed to be unanswerable, but it has a simple and certain answer, and that answer is "No." God's power is inexhaustible, and therefore no other power can overcome it; but all the power in the world cannot make a contradiction cease to be contradictory. As C. S. Lewis once said, "Nonsense does not become sense just because we put the words 'God can' in front of it."[1] To claim otherwise is to attempt to set God's power in opposition to His character, and to set oneself in opposition to both. For Scripture is just plain blunt about a number of things God *can* not do: He cannot lie, He cannot sin, He cannot change or grow old and senile. Nothing is too hard for Him, but some things are impossible—not because his power is subject to any restraint imposed from without, for there is no one and no thing in a position to impose it; but simply because He is who He is.

Another way to put the same question is this: is right right because God commands it, or does He command it because it is right? Neither formula is really helpful. It seems little short of blasphemous to think of the Holy One as merely a bare, omnipotent, and arbitrary will; but neither does right exist apart from him as a standard to which He could conform. It would not even be completely wise (though better than the other two alternatives) to say that God's power is "subject" even to his own character. It is the *expression* of his character; it is his character in action. He is not *subject* to logic, nor to the moral law, but He is the source of both. Neither character nor command, principle nor power, disposition nor decree is prior in Him, for He is eternal; but all are coordinated, for He is One. As He himself out it, He just *is*: "I Am that I Am." And what his character calls for and his will decrees, his power can accomplish; the zeal of the Lord of Hosts will perform it.

PRAYER: Father, for Thy pleasure were all things created, and so that all flesh may begin to see Thy Glory revealed, Thou fillest heaven and earth with Thy works. May I ever praise Thee for the made thing I am and for that of Thy Glory which awaits its imaging forth in me. Amen.

Factorem Coeli et Terrae
"Maker of Heaven and Earth"

In the beginning, God created the heavens and the earth ... and God said, "Let there be light." And there was. The very first thing we learn about God from the pages of Scripture is that He is creative; the second is that He is articulate, and that speech is the mode of his creativity. He speaks, and things which have never been before spring into existence. He speaks again, and they become differentiated, ordered, inter-related, impregnated with meaning and value. Evening and morning make Day, and it is good; every living thing brings forth its own kind, and it is good. The heavens declare his glory and the firmament shows forth his handiwork, as every syllable He has uttered rings out that He is: "I Am what I Am."

Even today, even with the distortions introduced by Sin, his invisible attributes and creative power are still clearly seen in what He has made. As best we can tell, it really is a *uni-verse,* a "one-song" place, with the same laws governing its behavior on Arcturus as on Earth, the same forces spinning the Milky Way as the Solar System and the Hydrogen Atom. Thus the continuing resonance of his creative Word declares his unity to all those with ears to hear. And yet this one-song place swarms with an innumerable multiplicity of individual notes, an infinite diversity of particular things. From the measureless and far-flung galaxies to the motes that people the sun's beam, from quarks and quasars to the quirks of individual personalities, from mountains to molecules and from ants to aardvarks and zooplankton to zebras, He makes it plain that His unity contains and fosters an incomprehensible richness of diversity. Hopkins praised Him for a full catalog of "dappled" and "fickle" points of loveliness which "He fathers forth, whose beauty is past change,"[2] showing that he had gotten the message: the seemingly contradictory appearances of unity and diversity in the world are *both* ultimately real, finding their roots and their resolution in the character of the Creator who is One God yet Three Persons yet One.

The world is indeed a created thing—it is in fact an artifact—and this truth tells us much about both the Maker and the made. Every physical fact is a natural symbol of some spiritual truth, a word from the Word, no less, and Scripture is the Rosetta Stone which lets us decipher the language whose speech is not heard but whose lines go out to all the earth (Ps. 19:1). And what does this language tell us? That He who contains and controls the vast interstellar distances is concerned for the fall of a sparrow; that stars and sparrows exist, at least in part, to the end that they might invest such theological affirmations with a meaning authorized from above and accessible to our minds; that our minds exist, at least in part, that the creative Word spoken from the beginning might be heard and understood.

Sin and its effects are the Satanic static which the enemy of our souls uses to try to obscure, if not blank out, the message. In the Fall he enlisted the Race in his efforts, so that apart from God's grace we add our puny voices to the din, trying to drown out the very Word which gives us our identity and reason for being. Our proximity to (and involvement in) this noise makes it appear to us a cacophonous, infernal buzzing indeed; but from a cosmic perspective it amounts to little more than a few bumblebees attempting to overpower the roar of Niagara Falls. For He *is* the Creator of heaven and earth, the source of all life, even of that which futilely tries to oppose Him, and which could not exist even to carry out its rebellion without his permission. We might wish that permission had never been granted, but it does preserve our own significance while giving rise to the context in which the Word spoken at creation might be uttered once again with an even deeper note and profounder meaning as the Word of redemption which was made flesh and dwelt among us.

PRAYER: Father, to show me the distance of Thy thoughts from mine, Thou madest the heavens. To show me the nearness of Thy sustaining benevolence, Thou madest the earth. To show me the part I have in both, Thou givest me the reconciling Word. May that Word be heard and done in me while it is yet Today. Amen.

Visibilium Omnium
"And All Things *Visible* and Invisible"

That God is Creator is one of the great cornerstones of all Christian doctrine. It is the first truth the Bible reveals about Him, and from that one fact can be derived most of his attributes, including the three famous "*omnis.*" If He created the heavens and the earth, then space, matter, and energy are all his inventions, things he thought up and spoke into being. There was a period when He was but they were not. Thus, his life is not contained in space as ours is, but rather space is contained in his life—He was there before space was; hence, *omnipresence*. The same thing could be said of his relationship to time (hence *eternality*) and to energy (hence *omnipotence*). Nothing exists which He did not design, and since He contains both space and time, nothing can escape his notice—hence, *omniscience*. In the absolute and unbridgeable distinction between Creat*or* and creat*ed* is the basis for *transcendence* and *holiness*; in his causal relationship with the cosmos we see the seeds of *immanence*. Creation is an act of giving and sustaining on which evil can only be parasitic; hence his *goodness*. Creation also entails ownership and *sovereignty* over what one has created. If God created the heavens and the earth and all that is in them, then these rights on his part extend to everything that is. And so basic and foundational are these truths that the fathers, having stated them adequately in the phrase "heaven and earth," wisely reiterated them by specifying that "*all* things" were included, those that are "visible" and those that are "invisible" as well.

"*Visibilium omnium*": He created all things visible, everything we can see—by implication, everything we can hear, taste, smell, or feel as well. Everything which can be detected by the more finely tuned and sensitive instruments we use to extend the range of our senses is also included: the whole physical universe from the galaxy cluster to the electron is his creation and hence his domain and his property. He conceived it in the whole and in the part, He designed it, He made it, and He maintains it in existence. He knows the vast sweep of its cosmic vistas and every nook and cranny of its hidden recesses in intimate detail. He understands perfectly every law and principle of its nature and operation, having written them all himself out of the infinite reservoirs of his rationality and his wisdom. Apart from His unflagging interest in this world, it would immediately cease to exist. He is the Maker of heaven and earth, and specifically of all things visible.

What an insult it is then to think of Him, as people often do, as the "God of the gaps." When people did not understand the mysteries of nature, we are told, they invoked the concept of a divine Being to explain what was otherwise inexplicable. But with the advance of science, the gaps in our knowledge began to shrink, and so did the domain of the mysterious in which the divine Power could be conceived to operate. The end result of the process is the secularization of the world, with God having been banished to a nebulous realm of the "spiritual" which has little relevance for the conduct of life in the material world ruled by science.

How foolish! As if the advances of physics had not revealed a world even *more* mysterious than we had thought. As if, even much more significantly, the advance of science had ever or *could* ever explain away the reality of God. Suppose *all* the gaps filled in and the mechanisms of nature cataloged and explained exhaustively; we still would not have answered the question why there is any mechanism to operate at all. The reductionism of the God of the gaps mentality is only a *reductio ad absurdum* which of necessity self-destructs in its own logical fatuity. The Church has always known better, and thus confesses Him as the Maker of heaven and earth and of all things visible *and* invisible. In so doing, we express the realization that his claims, his interests, and his sovereignty cannot be excluded from any area of life. Nor would we wish to exclude them if we could, for He is also the Father almighty, the Father of our Lord Jesus Christ. And that indeed is the wonder beyond all wonders and the glory of glories.

PRAYER: Father, Thy works teach me that beautiful is not beautiful unless it is also good and that good falls short of good unless it is also true. Help me so to occupy myself with all Thy creatures that my life may teach in turn what they teach me. Amen.

Et Invisibilium
"And All Things Visible *and Invisible*"

"The things which are seen," said Paul, "are temporal; the things which are unseen are eternal" (2 Cor. 4:18). He spoke not of things too small or too distant to be observed with the naked eye, but of another class of beings altogether than those which make up the physical universe. A host of Realities surrounds us which will not react to any agent in a test tube and which microscopes and telescopes are equally impotent to bring into focus—but he would be an impoverished soul indeed who denied their existence on that account. Scripture speaks of spiritual Intelligences and Powers which populate the heavens and roam the earth, some servants of God and friendly to Man, others hostile, the implacable enemies of both. It implies a non-material component of our humanity, capable of being absent from the body yet present with the Lord and of being reunited with a transformed and restored body at the Resurrection. And in addition to these spiritual beings there are the grand intellectual Realities: truth, goodness, beauty, justice, love. None of these things can be detected by microscopes, telescopes, radar, or CAT-scans. Are we therefore to think they are nothing more than mere words, abstractions arbitrarily put together from our experience of material things? No. They exist in the mind of God, and therefore they exist in reality. The unseen world as much as the seen then either was made by Him or flows from Him, the maker of *all* things, visible and invisible.

The Bible contrasts faith, interestingly, not with knowledge but with *sight* (2 Cor. 5:7). Faith is the ability to grasp the reality of the unseen in a world which has capitulated to the body's natural preference for the data it supplies the mind via the senses. We *see* the prosperity of the wicked and the suffering of the righteous, but we cannot see the glory which is to be revealed in us, with which the sufferings of the present life are not worthy to be compared. We see the dead body lying motionless in the casket and being lowered irrevocably into the earth, but we cannot see the spirit ascending to be with Christ until the Resurrection. We see day after day passing without change, but we cannot see the Day of His return drawing ever closer. And what we *do* see, we see day after day, day after day, over and over again and again in a constant and uninterrupted pounding rhythm until what we *see* begins to define reality for us. We think we have good reasons for believing in the unseen world and we stubbornly cling to our conscious orthodoxy, but without realizing it we unconsciously surrender to the tyranny of sight and begin to live as if the materialist's views were true. And the distance from this unconscious "practical atheism" to conscious overt apostasy is short, the path smooth, the steps few and easy.

How then do we combat this insidious encroachment of materialism? What weapons could avail against such subtle and powerful forces as these which threaten to deprive us of half our patrimony? (For Man *is,* as Thomas Browne reminds us, that "great amphibium," designed to live simultaneously in both worlds.)[3] There is only one. If faith is the ability to grasp the unseen in a world dominated by the senses, then "faith cometh by hearing, and hearing by the Word of God" (Rom. 10:17). Against all these machinations of the Enemy, against all this tyranny of sight, the Apostle Paul dares to oppose just one thing: the Word of God. And is it enough? Well, has it not stirred your heart and quickened your soul and worked its secret work in you before now? If you are a Believer it has, and if you are not it can, for it is quick and powerful and sharper than any double-edged sword (Heb. 4:12). We *will* be exposed to the incessant and strident voices of the senses, and for the wonders of the world they reveal we should glorify God, who made them. But lest the senses seem to monopolize our attention, we must deliberately stay in touch with the Word which comes to us from beyond the world of the material and the temporal. Only thus will we continue to believe at the deepest levels that the Creed so perceptively teaches us: He is the Maker of heaven and earth *and*—they were wise to reiterate it—*all* things, visible and invisible.

PRAYER: Father, the reward of seeking Thee is to discover that which needs a clearer vision than the body's eye and a more acute hearing than the body's ear. Make me to exercise those senses by which I have access to the things of Thy Kingdom. Amen.

II

THE SON

Et in unum Dominum
"And in one Lord"

The multiplicity in the unity of the Godhead is not merely a redundancy. Each member of the Trinity relates to us in a different way, specified by the primary designation He receives. The First Person is most fundamentally the Father, not only to the Second Person but to us as well. It is because He is who He is that we pray to God as our *Father* in Heaven. In relation to Him, the second Person is most basically the Son, modeling for the way in which *we* should ideally relate to the Father. As He relates to us, the Second Person is given many titles, explicit or implied: Friend, Brother, Teacher, Savior, Healer. But above all else He is supremely *Dominus, Kurios,* Lord.

This is not the merely political label it seems. Nor is it more cold or distant than the apparently more personal Friend or Brother. To hear this word as the saints of old must have heard it we must recapture in our imaginations the resonance it would have had for people who knew masters, kings, or tribal chieftains as something more than characters out of storybooks. We must learn to hear in it once again the fierce mixture of pride, gratitude, and devotion which the thane or knight felt toward the feudal lord to whose open-handed generosity he owed everything that he was in life. We must connect it once again with the humility of the good and faithful servant who is fulfilled to the marrow of his bones by the sound of pleasure in his master's voice when it pronounces those blessed words, "Well done!" We must reinvest ourselves with the spirit of Kent as he explains his devotion to king Lear by saying, "There is that in his countenance which I fain would call master."[1] If some of the examples I have chosen are anachronistic, the feeling they portray is not. The blessings of democracy are great, but the price is high if it includes the inability to comprehend what could lead a strong man spontaneously and wholeheartedly to prostrate himself before another, offer him the hilt of his sword, and desire to be commanded—to say, "my Lord."

For this indeed is a Lord of lords. Power and gentleness, glory and humility in all their fullness meet and are reconciled in his brow. He knows the authority of Command and yet is so secure in his dignity that he is able without embarrassment to wash the disciples' feet. He is the kind of Lord that men would gladly follow into the jaws of lions or the flames of torture—and many have. His life and His character give meaning to the usually empty phrases with which we address our merely human potentates: your majesty—my liege—your grace. Simply and plainly, the early Church had it right when they summed up everything that He was to them. *Kyrios Christos*: Christ is Lord.

He is Lord *by nature*: He "thought it not robbery to be equal with God" (Phil. 2:6).

He is Lord *by name*: "And His name shall be called Wonderful Counselor, the Mighty God, the Everlasting Father, the Prince of Peace" (Is. 9:6).

He is Lord *by right*: "Moses verily was faithful in all His house as a servant ... but Christ as a Son over His own house" (Heb. 3:5–6).

He is Lord *by reason*: "And Paul, as his manner was, went in unto them and three Sabbaths reasoned with them out of the Scriptures, opening and alleging that Christ must needs have suffered and risen again from the dead; and that this Jesus, whom I preach unto you, is Christ" (Acts 17:2–3).

He is Lord *by desert*: "Worthy is the Lamb who was slain to receive power and riches and wisdom and strength and honor and glory and blessing" (Rev. 5:12).

He is Lord *by decree*: "Therefore let all the house of Israel know assuredly that God hath made that same Jesus, whom ye crucified, both Lord and Christ" (Acts 2:36).

He is Lord *by destiny*: "That at the name of Jesus every knee should bow, of things in heaven, and in the earth, and under the earth; and that every tongue should confess that Jesus Christ is Lord, to the glory of God the Father" (Phil. 2:10–11).

Is He *your* Lord?

PRAYER: Father, these days museums house the relics of crowns, scepters and thrones. But Thou holdest Thy court in living hearts, and there, with Thy own, I still bow and still swear fealty to Thee, the Lord of All. Amen.

Et in unum Dominum, Iesum
"And in one Lord, *Jesus*"

"You shall call His name Jesus," said the Angel, "for He shall save his people from their sins" (Matt 1:21). It was a name of ancient and honorable lineage before it came to Him. *Jeshua*: the Hebrew word meant Savior, Rescuer, Hero—particularly, *Yahweh* saves, God rescues, the Lord is our hero. Joshua had borne that name with distinction as the captain of the Lord's armies in the conquest of Canaan and the occupation of the Promised Land, exemplifying and reinforcing both aspects of its meaning: it was Joshua who *delivered* Israel because he and Caleb had followed the Lord their *God* fully. So ever after it would be a name of honor in the nation, much the same as a modern American naming his son for Washington, Lee, MacArthur, or Schwarzkopf. It was a name of ancient and honorable lineage even before it came to Him, but when He had done with it, it would be a name above every name—for at the name of Jesus every knee will bow in heaven and on earth (Phil. 2:10–11). And thereby hangs a tale.

Gabriel conferred the name of Jesus on this child because it was his destiny to be a Deliverer with a difference: He would save his people from their sins. They were looking for a hero who would unite them against the Roman oppressor, throw off the yoke of Caesar, and restore the kingdom to its Davidic pride and Solomonic splendor; but they got more than they bargained for. This hero had subtler chains to shatter, a more deadly foe to conquer, and a deeper deliverance to offer. So naturally, his unimaginative countrymen in their undying gratitude spat on Him, stripped Him naked, and nailed Him to a stake of wood.

Their reaction should not surprise us; it did not in fact surprise Him. Most people object rather strenuously to being saved from their sins. What? Be delivered from the path of least resistance? Be set free from the settled conviction that I am the center of the universe? Be released from the confidence that I am in control of my fate and adequate in myself to please God with my own native virtue? Be liberated from my addiction to the self-indulgent habits which my flesh has come to dote on in spite of the knowledge that they are slowly destroying me? Be saved from my endless preoccupation with my rights, my lusts, my pride, my way, my glory? No, I would much rather string you up on the nearest gallows, thank you very much. You just mind your own business and leave me and my sins bloody well alone!

That is a reaction which, in the self-destructive perversity of our folly, we can all identify with—which is to say we are all sinners. In our saner moments, under the influence of the Holy Spirit or even of conscience, we recognize that it is leading us down the garden path which ends in futility, corruption, meaninglessness, death, and Hell; it mounts an insuperable barrier between us and everything which is beautiful, good, or true. But we cannot help ourselves, and so we need to be saved from our sins: from the guilt of them, the effects of them, the judicial penalty they deserve, and from the very suffocating attitude which is the essence of them and which in the insufferable arrogance of its rebellion against our good and gracious King merits and entails all the ugly consequences which follow them.

The very essence of the Christian Gospel is this: that Man was created good but rebelled against his Maker and fell into sin; that while we were yet sinners God loved us and gave his Son for us; that He came to bear our sins for us—their punishment and their essence—thereby setting us free from sin and death and making us heirs with Him of eternal life; that precisely because He came to do that, He experienced to the full the natural reaction which sin has against goodness; and that his Death exhausted all that sin was or deserved or could do, so that we can be set free of it if we embrace that Death through faith. Nothing less than the power of that ultimate Sacrifice could have paid sin's penalty and purchased our pardon, nothing less could have reversed the spiritual death it works in us, and nothing less could have broken the hold it has on us which keeps us even from wanting to be released. But it did and it does, for the One who died on that cross was *Jesus*, and He saves his people from their sins.

PRAYER: Father, Thy purposes are never thwarted, but all Thou hast promised, Thou givest in Thy Son. He came to rescue the Promised Land of fallen Humanity from itself, making of us a dwelling place for Thee forever. May what remains hostile to Him in me quickly and unconditionally surrender to Him. Amen.

Et in unum Dominum, Iesum Christum
"And in one Lord, Jesus *Christ*"

Jesus was a man who raised a lot of disturbing questions. The disciples kept asking themselves, "What manner of man *is* this?" (e.g, Lk. 8:25) and getting answers that would just not compute. That He was a man like themselves they could not doubt; they had seen Him eat and drink, sleep, and grow weary from overwork—so bone-tired that he slept right through a storm on the Sea of Galilee. But they had also seen Him heal the lame and blind, raise the dead, send demons screaming into the abyss with a word, and even silence the most ungovernable forces of Nature with a simple Command. What manner of man *is* this, that even the winds and the waves obey Him?

He gave them a chance to get their answers into focus by making the question explicit Himself. "Who do men say that I am?" Elijah, John the Baptist, one of the prophets come back from the dead. "But who do *you* say?" Peter took the bull by the horns: "Thou art the Christ, the Son of the living God." And Jesus thought the answer a good one: "Flesh and blood did not reveal this unto you, but my Father who is in Heaven" (Matt. 16:13–17).

"Thou art the Christ." Jesus was his name, Jesus Bar-Joseph in full, but Christ was his title. *Christos* in Greek translates the Hebrew *Meshiach*, Messiah: they both mean "Anointed One." The title ties Him in with a string of Old Testament national promises which may seem remote to his gentile followers two millennia later, but which were central to his mission and identity nonetheless.

Anointing with oil signified consecration to a task or office, and the supreme office for which it was used was kingship. The king was often referred to as "the Lord's anointed." And the promise had been given to David that his sons would sit on the throne of Israel forever. So when the dynasty—though not the line—was broken at the time of the Babylonian exile, the nation's hopes became focused on the Promise of a great Son of David who would arise with a special anointing from God to restore the kingdom to Israel. Peter's confession was that Jesus was precisely the promised Anointed One, the *Christos,* the Messiah of Israel.

Jesus was rejected in that role by the Nation because his concept of the Kingdom He had come to restore transcended the petty national interests of the Jewish people. He insisted on coupling the idea of Messiahship or Christhood with older and more foundational strands of the OldTestament Promise: that Abraham would be in his seed a bearer of blessing for *all* nations; that Eve in her seed would bruise the head, not of the Roman Eagle but of the Hellish and Edenic Serpent. That the triumphant Messiah was first to be the Suffering Servant whose stripes would bring healing to all nations: this was an idea they could not stomach. So to keep it from happening, they handed Him over to the Romans on trumped-up charges for execution, thus ironically ensuring the enactment of the very prophecies they had sought to ignore. And so the Christ, the seed of David, fulfilled his destiny as the Seed of Abraham and the Seed of the Woman—and of God Himself, as Peter had said. The glorious kingdom would come through suffering and be open to all, and the Israel whose history gave birth to the King and whose rejection of Him gave birth to the Kingdom will be a part of it at last. And that is what we confess when with Peter we call Him the Christ, the Son of the living God.

PRAYER: Father, I thank Thee that amongst the sounding gongs and tinkling cymbals of this world's noise, there have been clear trumpet calls to make way for the last Word spoken from the beginning, and this Word I now receive with joy. Amen.

Filium Dei
"Son of God"

No one hath seen God at any time, John the Apostle tells us, but the only begotten Son, the Logos from the bosom of the Father, He hath declared Him (Jn. 1:18). He who has seen the Son has seen the Father (Jn. 14:9); That is the only way we *can* see the father without being annihilated. The Son reveals the Father, but the Father also reveals the Son, through the prophets, through his own Voice pointing him out at the Baptism and Transfiguration. They are mutually revelatory: God the Father is the kind of father who could sire such a Son, and God the Son the kind of son who would come from such a Father.

We have already defined the fatherhood of the Father in terms of the sonship of the Son. It remains to define the sonship of the Son in terms of the fatherhood of the Father. The biblical idiom "son of" means, among other things, "having the character of." Calling James and John *Boanerges*, the sons of thunder, meant that they were thunderous people: energetic, boisterous, uninhibited (Mk. 3:17). The Son of Perdition is a person irretrievably lost (Jn. 17:12). A Son of Stripes (Deut. 25:2) is a person who deserves a beating. A son of God would be a godly person—*the* Son of God, uniquely begotten before all time, would be divine, an implication the Nicene fathers spelled out in unavoidable detail.

Jesus was then the Son of the God who imagined the universe, designed its laws, and called it into existence out of nothing with the power of his Word. He is the Son of the God who made creatures and taught them to multiply, as the four and five thousand eaters of loaves and fish would discover. He is the Son of the God who made a creature of clay in his own image and breathed into it the breath of life, as Jairus, the widow of Nain's son, and Lazarus would discover. He is the Son of the God who drove that creature from the Garden when it rebelled and fell into sin, but did not destroy it as it deserved; who, when he did destroy the increasingly corrupt offspring of that creature by a great flood, took pains to preserve a remnant of it alive, as people like the woman taken in adultery would discover.

Jesus is also the Son of the God who heard his people when they cried out in bondage and sent them a deliverer, who slew the firstborn of their oppressors but passed over those who were covered by the sprinkled blood of sacrifice. He is the Son of the God who brought them out of Egypt by his strong right arm, parted the Red Sea for them, and gave them the words of life in the smoke and thunder of Sinai. He is the Son of the God who let a whole generation's bones bleach in the desert sun when they refused his leadership at Kadesh Barnea after seeing such great signs.

Jesus is, in other words, the Son of the God who is wise and powerful, who is holy and righteous but compassionate and slow to anger, who will have mercy on the humble and penitent but who has no tolerance for self-righteousness and hypocrisy. Yes, that *does* sound like Jesus, doesn't it? *Filium dei*, undoubtedly his Father's Son, as lame, blind sinners and upstanding Pharisees would, in different ways, discover.

It boils down to this: We can have hope of being sons and daughters of this God because of the Fact that this Man, Jesus of Nazareth, was *the* Son of this God. Because Jesus is the Son of that Father—and the Father is the Father of that Son—we *want* to be sons and daughters of this God. And that is what we affirm when we confess that he is *Filium dei*, the Son of God.

PRAYER: Father, is there still disappointment in His Voice when He asks how long we can be with Him without seeing Thee in Him? Subdue the easy, the glib, the too-cozy images I have of Him. May Thy Holy Spirit reveal the majesty of Thee in Him and Him in Thee to my God-parched soul. Amen.

Unigenitum
"Only Begotten"

Well, then, Jesus is the Son of God. And I am a son of God, for Jesus gives to those who believe in him the right to become sons—and daughters too (Jn. 1:12). But there is a difference.

I am a son by adoption; Jesus is a son by nature. My sonship is derivative; his is original. Mine might not have been; his has always been. Mine is a gift; his is a right. We are both sons, but he is the only *begotten* Son—or, as it could be translated, uniquely begotten: *unigenitum*.

The Creed's affirmations about the Son constitute the longest of the four sections (Father, Son, Spirit, Church) largely so they can spell that uniqueness out beyond any possibility of confusion. Ninety-nine of the 167 words in the whole creed (59%) are thus devoted to the Son. At least twenty-three of those ninety-nine words (one-fourth) are devoted to specifying wherein lies the uniqueness of his begetting. It was *before all worlds*; he was begotten, *not made*. The fathers coined new words for it (*consubstantial*). They must have considered it extremely important.

It would not be a bad definition to say that a Christian is a person who worships the man Jesus of Nazareth as God. Then as now, there were numerous people who had a hard time understanding—or believing—how the infinite God could be present not just *in* but *as* a finite, flesh-and-blood human being. Indeed, it takes some believing. The easy way out is to say that Jesus wasn't really a man (the Docetists) or that he was something less than God—whether a little less (the Arians) or a lot less (modern liberals). Or, we could say that his divinity was like that of every human being, only more obvious (pantheists, transcendentalists, new agers). These are all much easier to imagine, and thus believe, and thus they would all be very sensible and common-sense solutions—if only they fit the facts.

Throughout the Gospel records, people kept asking, "What manner of man *is* this?"—who multiplies dead fish; who commands winds and waves, diseases and demons; who teaches with authority; who forgives the sins of other people; who makes fools of the Pharisees; who brings the dead to life and even more miraculously makes them feel their lives are worth the living—but who also gets so physically bone tired that he sleeps through a storm on the sea of Galilee? He turns water into wine, but he gets thirsty and has to ask for a drink. He is so powerful that he can command the most unruly of the elements, yet so weak that he needs help even to die. What manner of man *is* this?

All of the normal answers just did not compute, and all of the easy solutions left something out of the equation. The only answer that salvages our honesty and our rationality—if not, in the eyes of some, our sanity—is that he *was* the uniquely, only begotten Son of God in human flesh.

To miss that is to miss the glory, the romance, and the reality of Jesus. And while modern people may not relate well to technical terminology (which is strange, since they generate so much of it to much less purpose than that which is here), the phrases that follow are here to keep us from missing just that.

PRAYER: Father, all begettings trace the truth that God begets God: from I Am issues I Am. How, then, did the Eternal One so clothe Himself to be able to say, "I Am He that liveth and was dead; and, behold, I Am alive for evermore?" Enable me to go past what I cannot imagine to simply believe. Amen.

Ex Patre Natum
"Borne of the Father"

For the purposes of his sojourn on earth, Jesus was born to a Jewish peasant couple—the newlyweds Joseph and Mary—probably a few years before the "official" dawn of the Christian era. For the purpose of highlighting the fact that he was a fresh start for the human race, not just another ratification of Adam's rebellion like the rest of us, he was borne to a virgin. But before any of these births, he was borne to—li terally, *from*—God the Father. Every birth is a wonder and a mystery, but this one was the granddaddy of them all.

I was privileged to be present at the birth of both of my children. In both cases I did little more than encourage their mother and stand around in open-mouthed awe. But I did notice a thing or two about the process. Birth is not the beginning of life. In physical births like the ones I witnessed and like the one Jesus had at Bethlehem, the body has already been living for nine months. The birth is simply the *revelation* of a life which so far has lain hidden but now begins to assert itself in a new way.

In the case of Jesus being borne of the Father, too, the beginning of his existence is not the issue. There was no time when the Son was not the Son, borne of the Father. This begetting and birth are not in time at all, as we shall see. The point is that the Son relates to the Father as one borne: as the hidden life of God made manifest for all the world to see, asserting itself in a way that makes the whole universe sit up and take notice.

There has always been in the inscrutable life of God something that wants to emerge from hiding, to take on an independent life and existence while still remaining one with its Source. God is, in other words, eternally both Begotten and Begetter. Perhaps it was this impulse which led to a physical creation in the first place; certainly the Father creates through the Son, who thus represents the divine urge for externalization (Jn. 1:3).

Of course, the Son is not, like the rest of us, a *product* of God's drive to create: he is that drive, so fully and radically realized that in Jesus it actually became a part of creation while still remaining its Source. And his human birth is the place where the grand paradox of his divine origin becomes most striking: that the omnipotent Creator should become as helpless as a newborn baby, and, before that, a fetus, even an embryo. The old medieval Christmas play captures it well: "*Stabulo ponitur qui continent mundum,*" "He is placed in a stable who contains the world."[2] As God, borne of the Father, he still contained the world. As man he had entered that world so far as to be contained by it—yea, by a stable, a manger, the arms of a peasant girl. Only familiarity has dulled the wonder and the fascination contained in both Creche and Creed: if you thought it was true you would have to fall to your knees in worship.

There is in God, then, a Reality of which physical birth is a faint and distant echo but which one particular physical birth reveals in blazing glory. That Reality has a name, and the name is Jesus, who was borne of a virgin because first He was borne of the Father.

PRAYER: Father, like green plant yielding seed after its kind, so God yielded God after His kind, full of grace and truth. May I so receive Thee through Him that I, too, may come to be that which is after Thy kind. Amen.

Ante Omnia Saecula
"Before All Ages"

Jesus was borne of the Father *before all ages,* or before all worlds, as it is sometimes translated—before the beginning of time, or before creation, in other words. There was never a moment of time when God's drive for self-expression was not exerting itself, coming to birth as a second center of personal consciousness in the Godhead but distinct from the Father. Theologians call this truth "the eternal generation" of the Son. God has always been bringing forth the Son, and the Son has always been coming from the Father. There is no such thing as a time before this process—which may be said to be just another name for the life of God—had begun.

Why did the Nicene fathers stress this fact in their long elaboration on the uniqueness of the Son's begetting? It was partially because for us birth is a process but also an *event,* which begins with the onset of labor and ends with the cutting of the umbilical chord and the first wailing breath of life. We come from our parents but also leave them, and become not only separate and distinct persons but also different beings. But the Son's birth from the Father was not an event in time but a dynamic relationship in the Godhead that existed prior to time and is not dependent on it.

We are therefore reminded that birth is an *analogy* for the Son's relationship with the Father, one filled with profound significance for us, but not one to be pressed too far. It is a divinely authorized word picture intended to give us some concept of what is ultimately unpictureable. We are right to use it, and it would be disobedient to discard it. But we are also reminded that, as much a mystery as physical birth remains to us, the life of God is something far more incomprehensible. The language gives us a measure of understanding that is true as far as it goes, but it is designed to communicate awe as much as information.

A reason more immediately pressing in the minds of the fathers was the need to guard the uniqueness of Jesus from errors which were attractive to the people of their day. The Arians were people of stubborn common sense who insisted on taking the metaphor of birth literally, as an event that had happened in time. This made the Son less than eternal, a being who had a beginning—hence less than fully God. Thus they avoided the intellectual difficulties which accompany the doctrines of the Trinity and the Incarnation. God was simply the Father, and it was a great but finite and created Spirit that joined itself to human nature—all much simpler and easier to believe.

Except that if you *do* locate the begetting of the Son in time, you create other complications: like what Jesus could have meant by saying, "Before Abraham was, *I am*" (Jn. 8:58). Or what John meant by saying that in the beginning, the Word *already was* (Jn. 1:1)—as the Greek verb can be accurately translated. Or by saying that the Word spoken by God was both with God and *was* God.

Simplicity is an intellectual virtue, but not at the price of ignoring the facts. And one very important one is that the Son was begotten *ante omnia saeculae*: before the ages of time began.

PRAYER: Father, as fish for the water and birds for the sky, so Thou art making us to be native to Thy eternity. Grant that our present groaning in Time may prod us to keep remembering that for which we were made. Amen.

Deum de Deo
"God of God"

At this point, the Creed becomes, by modern standards, almost a bit tedious. By now the full deity of the Son who was incarnate as the man Jesus has been sufficiently established by the fact that his begetting in the Godhead occurred before time. So why belabor it? God of God, light of light, very God of *very* God. We get the point already!

Well, I don't know that it is really possible to *belabor* so important a truth as the deity of our Savior. But it is possible—and desirable—to *savor* it, which is what the Creed here gives us an opportunity to do.

God of God: the nuance emphasized here is carried by the simple preposition *of*. The idea was present in the relationship between Begetter and Begotten already, but the new phrase gives it a nicely compact resonance. The Son is both God himself and *of* God the Father: derived from him, coming from him, sent by him. He is the Word, the expression of the Father's mind, focused outward toward us in grace and looking back to him in love. He is the Other implied in the royal we of Genesis, when God says not "I think I will" but "Let *us* make Man in our image." He is God of God like He is Lord of lords and King of kings: the ultimate God, thoroughly God, as God as you can get. He is the Son who comes forth from the Father and returns to him, taking us with him if we are united to him by faith.

The deity of Christ is worth lingering over not only because God is the most exalted and worthy object of contemplation but also because God *of* God means God *for* us—and *with* us and ultimately *in* us as well. It might be easier to believe that a creature begotten in time could become a man, but then why bother to believe it at all? No matter how great and powerful, no matter how *like* God, it would not *be* God.

The Christian faith claims that it was God himself who became one of us, who called himself our friend, who lived our life and died our death, who replaced Adam as the rightful head of our race, and who now represents our interests at the Father's right hand in the throne room of Heaven. That is why we can know God as our Father and Friend and Liege. Anything less would not be enough—for no matter how high we might be raised by union with something less than God, the gap between finite and infinite, creature and Creator, would remain unbridged. We could still only worship him from afar—and it would still be a great distance indeed, for a trillion is no nearer infinity than a thousand.

The Gospel—the good news—is this: that when we come to know God in Christ, we come to know *God*: God of God, light of light, very God of very God. Nothing less. Believe it if you can; doubt it if you must; but if you water it down, you betray us all and make humanity less than it was created to be. For we will have no truck with messengers, viziers, press secretaries, or any other such bureaucratic substitutes. Because of who Jesus is, we will walk past them all, right up to the throne of the One we call Abba, Father. No angel, cherub, or seraph will come before us. To the Arians and their modern successors, the Nicene fathers say, in effect, "Sirs, stand aside. We would see Jesus."

PRAYER: Father, He Whom Thou sent and He alone is Ladder to Heaven and Door to the Fold. Grant that my life may be a song of ascent and an entering in both through and to Him. Amen.

Lumen de Lumine
"Light of Light"

God is light, says John, and in him is no darkness at all (I Jn 1:15). He is a consuming fire (Heb. 12:29). Even his angelic messengers appear in raiment that gleams like lightning (Lk. 24:4). And when they appear before his throne, where he dwells in unapproachable light (1 Tim. 6:16), even they have to veil their faces (Is. 6:2).

When Dante finally glimpsed the beatific vision, he saw "One Point ... so radiantly bright / So searing to the eyes it strikes upon / They must needs close before such piercing light" (*Paradiso* canto xxviii).[3] For Milton, light belongs in heaven and is so foreign to hell that there the very flames give off "No light, but rather darkness visible" (*Paradise Lost* I. 63).[4] And Henry Vaughn saw eternity as "A ring of pure and endless light / All calm as it was bright."[5] The ring was stable but dynamic, and its splendor something relevant to us: "This ring the Bridegroom did for none provide / But for his bride." In all this the poets have not departed from the biblical vision, for Jesus promised that we should share his glory (Jn. 17:22), indeed, that we will be clothed with the morning star (Rev. 2:28).

The phrase "light of light" is parallel with the phrase "God of God." As he is God coming forth from God without evacuating Heaven, so he is light coming forth from light without exhausting the light. He is the light that, coming into the world, enlightens every man (Jn. 1:9). That is, as the divine Reason in whose image we were created, it is owing to him that we have the capacity of knowing and understanding anything; and as the divine Word incarnate, it is owing to him that we have the opportunity of knowing God.

The contrast between darkness and light is part of the framework on which the biblical vision is constructed. Thus Christ is linked with kindled lamp, blazing star, rising sun, with all that is healthy and wholesome and has no need to hide its head in shame. With him we stride with steady steps toward home; without him we stumble and fall and lead each other into various ditches. With him, the five wise virgins add their own lamps to the festal splendor of the marriage feast; without him the five foolish virgins are left in outer darkness—and the door is shut.

The problem is that God has sent the light into the world, but men love darkness because their deeds are evil (Jn. 3:19). We can hide in darkness, but the light would expose us for what we are. Yet if we are willing for that to happen, the same light also reveals everything that is good, true, beautiful, and worthwhile. If we stop hiding—if we stop pretending not to be evil, so we can become the recipients of grace—then we can walk in the light as *He* is in the light, and the blood of Jesus cleanses us from all sin (1 Jn. 1:7).

Light is positive, active, dynamic; darkness is negative, inert, impotent. In natural physics it is correct to say that darkness is the absence of light. It will not work to say that light is the absence of darkness, for darkness is not the presence of anything. In the physics of the Spirit, the same truth prevails: for the light shone in the darkness, and the darkness could not overcome it (Jn. 1:5). Such was the coming of the Son of man, who was also God of God and light of light.

PRAYER: Father, I bless thee for speaking the world's first light, for separating it from what was not light, and for the light of Thy glory in the face of Jesus Christ. Command Thou that light to shine in my heart and separate me from my own darkness so that I may behold Him unveiled and so be changed. Amen.

Deum Verum de Deo Vero
"Very God of Very God"

The insistent affirmations of the Son's full deity rise to a grand crescendo—or come to rest on the bottom line—or do both simultaneously, if you will—in the next phrase. The One who is God of God and Light of Light is *very* God of very God. It could be translated "true God of true God." Just in case anyone has missed it, in other words, we really do mean to say that the Being incarnate in Jesus of Nazareth was God.

And he is not just any God. He is the one *true* God, God with a capital G. The God of the beginning of the Creed, the Father Almighty who made Heaven and Earth and all things visible and invisible, is his Father, and he as the Son shares fully in his Father's divine nature. Thus the bottom line is that Jesus is truly God, the God of truth, the true God.

He is *truly God*. Not a little less, not a little other, not a divine-human hybrid: Jesus is really, truly *God*. He is just as truly human, and that is not an easy fact to hold together with this one, but neither is it now the point. As a man he was physically located, ignorant of the day and hour of his return, and capable of exhaustion. But as God, by virtue of his still-maintained personal rootedness in the ongoing life of the Trinity, he was omnipresent, omniscient, omnipotent. And he still is all those things. Jesus is truly God. You can worship him and it is not idolatry; you can pray to him and it is not blasphemy; you can present your body and soul as a living offering to *this* human being and it is not sacrilege. You can believe in him and your trust is not misplaced. He is very God of very God.

He is the *God of truth*. As human, Jesus could be surprised and confess his ignorance, but he never lied and he could not be misled. As God he cannot lie: His very character is the source of truth, the standard of truth, the basis for the existence of truth. He spoke of light and there was light, of firmaments and continents, grass and trees, birds and behemoths, and they all obediently sprang into place in reality just as He had said. He spoke the Ten Words to Moses in smoke and fire, and right and wrong have never before or since become more clear. He spoke through his servants the Prophets, and he did not speak in vain: Not one jot or tittle could pass away until all was fulfilled. His words in the days of his flesh could cut self-righteous Pharisees to the quick, bring hardened prostitutes to tears, and make the lame walk, the blind see, the dead live. His word defines reality. And he is still the God of truth, very God of very God.

He is *the true God*. The false gods are made by hands (or minds) and have to be carried about from place to place, but Jesus (as much as the Father) made the Heavens. The other gods are silent or speak through unintelligible oracles, but the parables of Jesus still put life in perspective. The other gods perform their great exploits in the inaccessible realm of mythological time, but *this* one sticks his neck out in the days of Caesar and Herod and Pilate. He is, as Dorothy L. Sayers put it, "the only God with a date in history."[6] He is the only true God, very God of very God indeed.

It cannot be overemphasized, stressed too much, or said too often: Christians are people who worship the *man* Jesus of Nazareth as *God*—because that is what he was. His deity is not to them a truth that is vague, mystical, "spiritual," or metaphorical. They take it in the plainest, barest, most literal sense possible, and they do not want you to miss it or misunderstand it. They mean us to understand that he was very God of very God. And in the Nicene Creed they are not through hammering it home even yet.

PRAYER: Father, Thou named Thyself, "I Am" and the mouth of Thy Son named Himself with Thee: "I am the Truth." Eradicate all pretense, all illusion, all deception in me by the Divine Fact of Thyself. Amen.

Genitum, non Factum
"Begotten, not Made"

The uniqueness of the Son's begetting by the Father lies, as we have seen, in the fact that it took place before time began while ours takes place in history; that it was inherent in the nature of God, while ours is contingent on His grace and good pleasure; that it was original while ours is derivative. His makes Him God of God; ours makes us human, and our spiritual begetting in the new birth makes us merely godly men and women. He is light of light; we are, in Him, enlightened. In sum, we were first *made* and then, as believers in Christ, spiritually reborn. He was begotten, *not made,* of one substance with the Father. Far from being made, He is in fact the Maker, along with the Father, of all things visible and invisible. Through Him all things were made that were made, and without Him nothing was made.

In the fundamental distinction between creature and Creator lies perhaps the clearest definition of what it means to say that Jesus is God. His human body was made at a point in time, then nourished and built up out of mother's milk and matzo bread, figs and dates and fatted calves, just like ours. But the Person joined to that body was the One who made out of nothing the very heavens and earth and all they contain. Other people's gods, Israel was constantly reminded, are made of wood and stone and have to be carried about from place to place; but Yahweh made the heavens.

Only God, after all, can truly *create.* We, made in His image, can do so after a fashion, in a way that transcends anything the other animals can do. But it remains a mere reflection of God's making. We can, through language and imagination, manipulate natural elements into new shapes and combinations. We can, as Sir Philip Sidney put it, make as it were "another nature," "far surpassing her doings."[7] But we remain mere tinkerers after all, unable to come up with anything so simple as a new primary color. We pile the blocks into some impressively intricate structures or carve them into Lincoln Logs or Tinker Toys, but Someone Else had to give us the wood. And we can saw it in two—always, in the process, losing some in sawdust—but only Someone Else can make *more.*

Our sovereignty over the wood, in other words, is real because we were made in the Maker's image, but limited because we, like it, were made. We are higher, being in God's image, but we and the blocks are fellow creatures after all. But where did we both come from, building blocks and blockheads together? *Someone* had to make the blocks. And if the Unmade Maker were among us as one of us, what might He do? Turn water into wine? Feed five thousand people with a handful of fish? Make the lame walk, the blind see, the dead live? Hmmm.

The Son was begotten, not made. *Begotten* distinguishes Him from the Father while affirming their oneness in kind. *Not made* distinguishes Him from the finite creation. Begotten, He is *with* God; not made, He *is* God: God of God, God for us.

"Not made" was, of course, one more slam at the Arians, who made the Son the highest of the creatures. It is still a useful handle on the concept of deity. Because the Son was begotten as opposed to made, in Him was life, and that life was the light of men. And because of that, the same life can be born in us. Because He was not made, it is infinite and inexhaustible and can thus be shared with and sustained in His finite creatures unendingly, without diminution at its source. For the Word became flesh and dwelt among us, and we beheld His glory, as of the only begotten of the Father, full of grace and truth.

PRAYER: Father, He that was born, not made, put on the made so that those made might receive power to become God-born sons and daughters. For Thy Son's sake, stir that new life within me so that Thy quickening power may permeate all I think, say, and do. Amen.

Consubstantialem Patri
"Of One Substance with the Father"

There is a modern strain of thought which holds that, in their laudable desire to defend the deity of Christ from contemporary attacks, the Nicene Fathers didn't know when to stop. In their polemic against the Arians, they supposedly got Christian theology off on the wrong foot, unintentionally transforming the dynamic personal God of the Old Testament into a Greek philosophical abstraction, more like Plato's Ideal or Aristotle's Unmoved Mover than the Yahweh of Sinai or the Jesus of Calvary. The place where this complaint surfaces most insistently is the place to which we have now come: the assertion that the Son was of one substance (*homoousion, consubstantial*) with the Father.

The statement does indeed assume knowledge of a set of Greek philosophical categories. A *substance* is the foundational, irreducible essence of a thing, that which makes it what it is. The opposite of a substance is an *accident*: an external characteristic of a thing that might have been different without—ahem—"substantially" altering its nature. In modern scientific terms, a change in accidents would be what we call a "physical change," affecting things like size or shape or density but leaving the same mix of elements; a change in substance would be like a "chemical change," which produces a whole new kind of matter from what was there before. One set of questions asks if something is big, little, round, or square; the other asks if it is gold or iron. So the Creed is saying that the Father and the Son are both gold.

To go back to the Greek way of saying it, I am human because I participate in the *substance* of humanity. I happen to have brown hair—but that is merely an *accident*. Some people have red hair, some blonde, some black. The substance is what makes them all human in spite of their surface differences. If my hair turned gray—or fell out (it's working on both processes, by the way)—it would not change the fact that I am a human being. Thus we might call *substance* "the reality below the surface." The Creed then claims that Jesus has such a reality and that it the same as the Father's.

So what is the problem? Well, I have a learned friend who doubts that such things as substances even exist. They might just be a name we made up so we could conveniently talk about a set of characteristics human beings (or chairs or chalices, ants or angels) happen to have in common. But there might be no actual *substance* that exists apart from all those individual humans, chairs, chalices, ants, and angels. (This position in philosophy is called *Nominalism* because it holds that substances and essences are just names, not real things.)

So, what if my friend is right? I personally think that it is possible—though not certain—that he is. It is at least an open question. Would this mean that in reciting the Nicene Creed we are tying the deity of Christ to a dubious philosophical concept that might blow up in our faces, destroying our faith in Jesus as God along with an outmoded Greek philosophy? An increasing number of people are afraid that it might.

I think, though, that there is another question equally worth asking: What were the Nicene Fathers trying to say with this language? And is it something we would still want to affirm, even if we would not now all choose to express it in the same categories?

Suppose you are a Nicene Father. All the intellectuals around you are used to talking about substances and accidents. You probably accept them yourself. So you naturally look for a way to express the central truth of the nature of Christ in terms of those categories. But nominalism versus realism (the philosophical position that substances are real) is not your main point. What is? That the Son and the Father are the same kind of Being, not different, not even similar, but the same. Their distinct persons are part of the same ultimate Reality which is the one and only God. Assuming for the sake of argument that substances exist, the Son's would be the same as the Father's. They share the same nature, which is Divine. If you have a problem with substances, fine: Just mentally translate it as "having the same nature as the Father" and pass on. For that the Father and the Son are identical in nature is essential to our affirmation of Christ's deity, and that, as we have seen, is essential to our faith that His death and resurrection save us by reuniting us with God. Don't loose the *substance* of what the Creed is trying to say, in other words, in the *accidents* of the categories through which it is trying to say it.

Well, look at that last sentence. It is hard, isn't it, to avoid using the language of substance? Even confirmed nominalists may find themselves saying that a position is *substantially* correct, or that a politician's speech sounded good but lacked *substance*. They are speaking metaphorically (as nominalists) when they borrow this language, but they still do find it useful. Let them therefore continue to use it with understanding when they confess that the Son is consubstantial with the Father.

PRAYER: Father, He prayed that we might share in the oneness of Thee and Him. Let the Divine Unity bring together by participation in Itself what remains disjointed in me, what remains dismembered among His body, and what remains subject to futility in His universe. Amen.

Per Quem Omnia Facta Sunt
"Through Him all Things were Made"

Scripture involves all three members of the Godhead in the act of Creation. The Spirit brooded over the surface of the waters when the world was yet formless and void (Gen. 1:2) and continues to give life to the physical creation, energizing what seems to be the inherent life-force of Nature (Ps. 104:30). Solomon personified Wisdom as a master workman who was with God in the beginning (Prov. 8:22–31), and John, with a strong allusion both to that passage and to Genesis 1:1, said that the *Word* was there, was with God, and that through Him all things were made, without Him, nothing. So before moving to the Son's role in the Redemption or Re-Creation of the world, the Creed reminds us of His stake in the original creation: through *Him* all things were made.

Dorothy L. Sayers gives the classic exposition of the Trinity's role in creation in *The Mind of the Maker*. She notes that, whatever else it may be, the Nicene Creed is an accurate account of the way the human mind works in creating. Every act of creation involves a central controlling *idea* (the Father), the *craftsmanship* that *incarnates* it in some concrete medium (the Son), and the *power* that flows from the first two (the Spirit) to move an audience. These, being separate and distinct functions, are yet one act of creation. So the classical theological statements about the Mind of the Maker are a psychologically accurate description of the mind of the maker made in His image when that mind is in operation. This we can verify empirically—which is what we would expect if we are indeed created in the image of the original Trinitarian Creator.[8]

If Sayers is right, we can see that the individual involvement of the members of the Trinity in creation—or or re-creation—is not redundant. The Father initiates, the Son accomplishes, and the Spirit applies. The Father proposes, the Son produces, and the Spirit promulgates. So also the

Father elects, the Son atones, and the Spirit emancipates. The Father predestines us to adoption, the Son propitiates, making possible justification and a restored relationship with God through faith, and the Spirit prepares us for faith and preserves and protects us in that faith.

The Son then is as creative as the Father, though perhaps representing a different aspect of the process of creation. The Son effects the enfleshment of the Father's ideas in the material world; He is the agent by which they become grounded in physical form. We see Him in His earthly ministry *making* wine out of water, thousands of fishes out of a handful, straight limbs out of crooked, new and healthy flesh out of leprous and necrotic, living bodies out of dead. We see Him *making* up stories on the spur of the moment to carry on his debates, stories that can never be forgotten. In the entire history of world literature, nobody can compete with him as a *maker*-up of parables; nobody even comes close. And it is little wonder, for He got his start helping the Father make galaxies and solar systems out of cosmic dust and cosmic dust out of nothing, all orchestrated by mathematical principles that they made up out of their own glorious minds.

C. S. Lewis points out brilliantly in *Miracles* how the mighty works of Jesus were like signatures, identifying Him clearly with the Father. Who can still the winds and the waves? Only the One who was ignorantly worshiped by pagans as Poseidon. Who can multiply grain to feed the masses? Only the One worshiped ignorantly by pagans as Ceres. Who can turn water into wine? Only the One worshiped ignorantly by pagans as Bacchus. Who really does all these things? Only the One worshiped truly by His chosen people as Yahweh. And He *always* does them, and He *alone* does them, though usually more slowly and using intermediate apparatuses like weather fronts, stalks of wheat, and grapevines. When Jesus does such things suddenly, immediately, and dramatically like God in the Beginning, He plants His flag and throws down His gauntlet in no uncertain terms, hanging out his shingle as the One through whom the Father made all things that ever came into being.

This is the One who for us and for our salvation came down from Heaven and was made man. That is where all this language has been going; and on the next page of this book, it will finally begin to arrive. [9]

PRAYER: Father, through Him the universe was spoken into existence, and then, dusty footed, He worked His wonders, small and local. Work now His re-making of us, His new world's beginning, small and local, in our hearts. Amen.

Qui Propter Nos
"Who for Us ..."

This great figure, the Son, who has the same nature as the Father Almighty, who with Him made all things visible and invisible, who is, like Him, a distinct and individual person while they are both yet one God—*this* great Being, no less, came down from Heaven and was made man. That is rather astounding. What is even more astounding is that He did it for us.

Scripture is quite plain about the fact that what ultimately motivates the mighty acts of God is zeal for his own glory. This is true of everything in general and of salvation in particular. "For the sake of my Name I delay my wrath," He declares, "... For my own sake, I will act; for how can my Name be profaned? And my glory I will not give to another" (Is. 48:9–11). Paul insists that God chose, predestined, and adopted us "for the praise of the glory of his grace"; He redeemed us through his blood, made known to us the mystery of his will, and gave us an inheritance so we "should be to the praise of his glory"; and He has sealed all that to us with the Spirit "to the praise of his glory" (Eph. 1:6, 12, 14). And Jesus himself, when steeling his soul to face the horrors of the Cross, prayed, "Father, the hour has come; glorify thy Son, that the Son may glorify Thee" (Jn. 17:1).

That God's deeds are finally driven by His own glory is perhaps the most profound truth He has revealed. It is important for us to grasp it for a number of reasons. One is that glad assent to it is the surest sign that we have finally given up our propensity for self-idolatry and are willing for God to be *God*. One is that the perspective it gives us is therefore the key to both spiritual depth and spiritual backbone. But another is that only a rock-solid rootedness in that perspective can provide the standpoint from which we can fully appreciate the subsidiary truth that comes to expression here: This self-contained and self-sufficient God whose own glory is not just *His* greatest good but *the* greatest good of all his creatures has stepped out of himself to give his only Son—*for us.*

He did it, as the most beloved verse in all of Scripture says, because He loved us so much (Jn. 3:16). He came, as Jesus himself explained, to seek and to save that which was lost, to serve rather than be served, and to give his life as a ransom for many (Lk. 19:10; Mt. 20:28). And, as the Apostle tells us in what may be the most astonishing verse in the Bible, "God demonstrates His love toward us in this, that while we were yet sinners, Christ died for us" (Rom. 5:8). He did not come for us as penitents, as his children, or as victims foreseen as deserving his help. He came for us as *sinners.* While we were still in love with ourselves, deliberately flouting his will and shaking our puny rebellious fists in his Face, stubbornly destroying everything He had built in his creation—it was *then* that He died for us. While we were in the very act of spitting in His Face and mocking Him in His distress, as his tendons pulled against the spikes and his torn back grated against the splinters, He looked down and said, "Father, forgive them, for they know not what they do" (Lk. 23:34).

For those who do not know the Son, the universe is a hostile and forbidding place. It seemingly casts us up out of the primordial chaos with aspirations for meaning, love, and fulfillment which it is utterly incapable of fulfilling. It might send us rain for our crops, but it would just as soon blow us away with a tornado or drown us in the sea or bury us in an earthquake. It really doesn't care which it does. It surrounds us with creatures as selfish as ourselves. If by some chance we find one who seems capable of loving us, our own self-centeredness and insensitivity will probably drive a wedge into the relationship which will eventually make it worse than hate. Or, if not, the universe will probably give one of us cancer. At best it will give us seventy or so fairly tolerable years and then slowly kill us while depriving us in the process of our last shred of dignity. Hobbes had it right when he said that in the state of nature life tends to be solitary, nasty, poor, brutish, and short. If nothing else, it will certainly be—by cosmic standards—short.

It is worth knowing that, in such a world, the world our sin has made, we are not alone. Some one came for us. Knowing us at our worst, He left glory unimaginable to join us, to be with us, to be one of us, to die for us.

Having ventured that much for us already, there can be no limit to his commitment. He came for us, and He *is* for us—He lives to make intercession for us (Heb. 7:25). And if *this* One is for us, then who can be against us?

No one that matters.

PRAYER: Father, we thank Thee for things that acquaint us with Thy glory: for fire and sun, for glowing skies, for strength of horse and man, for heights and depths. Take from our eyes the scales of self-absorption so that Thy glory may be the object of all our seeing. Amen.

Qui Propter nos Homines
"Who for us *Men*"

The Coming of Christ has relevance for all the creation which groans in travail, longing for its redemption (Rom. 8:22), and it is an event of cosmic significance that angels long to study (1 Pet. 1:12). But it was "for us *men*"—that is, for us human beings, supremely—that He came.

Even before that Coming, Scripture marveled at God's interest in humanity, its central place in His thoughts and purposes for the cosmos. "What is man that thou art mindful of him?" the Psalmist wondered. And he marveled that "Thou hast made him a little lower than the angels" (Ps. 8:4–5). It was Adam and Eve alone of all the animals God made who were made in His image. They alone were given the ability to step outside of instinct and *think* rationally, given the ability to generate language, made able to have fellowship with God and given by Him the task of ruling over the material creation. As God's governor, responsible for this planet (if not the whole physical universe), Adam's actions were crucial, affecting all other creatures. And the actions of his descendants continue to do so in ways they can no longer predict or control.

It was no accident that Adam (the Hebrew word not only for the first individual man but for all of mankind) was given this pivotal role. He was in fact precisely a little lower than the angels—and by the same token a good bit higher than any of the other animals. He was (and his descendants are), as far as we know, the only creatures in the universe who constantly participate in both the physical and the spiritual worlds. As such they are the unique bridge that holds both halves of creation together. We have bodies like the animals; we are spirits like the angels—a claim no other species can make. Sir Thomas Browne rightly called our race "that great and true *amphibium*, whose nature is disposed to live, not only like the other creatures in diverse elements, but in divided and distinguished worlds."[10]

For people created to fill such a grand and important role in the scheme of things, we might expect the Creator to venture much. But if to be human is to be part of a species entrusted with such a high calling and privilege, it is also to be part of one which has failed more miserably, wickedly, and inexcusably to be worthy of such exalted favors than any which can be imagined. To whom much is given, from them much is expected. By that criterion we are the worst, most despicable ingrates in the universe, rivaled only by the fallen angels themselves. We have been and remain sinners: not people who are imperfect, people who have made some mistakes, but hard-hearted rebels, traitors against a good and gracious King who gave us everything we had. We have earned His enmity, we deserve His disapproval, we revel in our rejection of Him, and we wear His wrath as if it were a badge of honor. We have scorned His messages, despised His long-suffering patience, stoned His prophets, and nailed His only Son to a stake of wood. And these are not just isolated incidents perpetrated by some of our ancestors, but the daily deluge of deeds that flows from the bent of our inmost natures. We are indeed the sons and daughters of our parents, and we show no signs of any amendment any time soon.

No one has ever summed up the heights and depths of our identity better than C. S. Lewis: "You come of the Lord Adam and Lady Eve," said Aslan. "And that is both honor enough to erect the head of the poorest beggar and shame enough to bow the shoulders of the greatest emperor on earth. Be content."[11] Knowing the fullness both of our glory and our degradation, knowing the worst of us, Christ not only came for us but became one of us. For that fact we can have nothing but awe; to that fact we can only respond in humble faith and adoration; and with that fact we must indeed rest content.

PRAYER: Father, we confess that we have wasted our inheritance. We thank thee for that disillusionment which is the scourings of our fallenness. Grant us an ongoing coming to our senses that ever bids us arise and come to Thee. Amen.

Et Nostram Salutem
"And for our Salvation"

Jesus came for us—for us men—*and* for our salvation. The Creed's indirection at this point contains a subtle profundity. It does not say that the Son came to save us, nor that He came for our salvation. It says that He came for *us*—and our salvation. He came for us human beings, the lost sheep and lost coin of his parables. And that fact brings with it *salutem*: health, well-being, salvation for us.

It is almost as if salvation—the benefit that accrues to us—is an afterthought, or, perhaps better, a byproduct of his coming. The main thing that He came for was us. It is good for the lost sheep that it be found, that it end up in a sheltered fold safe from wolves and cliffs and landscapes devoid of grass or still water. But the Shepherd went after it thinking not so much of how much better off the sheep would be after he found it as of the fact that it was His sheep and it was lost and He wanted it back.

The Creed then implies here what is explicit in many Scriptures: the radically personal nature of God's love for lost sinners. Jesus did not come into the world for an abstraction but for a people promised to Him by the Father and elected to that destiny from before the foundations of the world. He did not die to make salvation a theoretical possibility for any human potentially interested so much as to make it an actuality for a definite people already foreseen. When He went to the Cross, He was not thinking of anything as nebulous as the human race; He had his mind fixed on something as concrete and definite as you and me. He came for lost sheep—not just any lost sheep He happened to stumble across, but one that had my name and my face in His mind even before I was born.

What happens to lost sheep like us when he does come for us is *salvation*. Salvation is in Scripture a rich word comprehending all the benefits that accrue to us as a result of being found by the One who came for us. For this One happens to be the Source of Life; to be found by Him is to know life eternal, to pass from death to life.

Theologians have a number of technical terms for the various aspects of the treasure that is this life in Christ. Among them are *imputation, justification, sanctification, adoption, regeneration,* and *glorification.*

In *Imputation,* our sins are counted by God as Christ's so that His death on the Cross can be accepted as their payment, and His righteousness is counted as ours so that God can reestablish a relationship with us. This leads to *Justification,* in which God declares us righteous and pronounces us acquitted, innocent of all charges of sin because of Christ's sacrifice. From this flows *Sanctification,* the process of becoming in actuality what God has already declared us to be and accepted us as being in Justification, i.e., holy. With the barrier of sin thus removed in Justification, we are restored to a relationship with God in *Adoption,* as He takes us for His beloved sons and daughters. From the moment of Justification there is also *Regeneration,* the restoration of spiritual life in those who were dead in their trespasses to sins. And the end result of all this is *Glorification,* when God's redeemed people are confirmed in their redemption in Heaven with no possibility ever of falling again.

The lost are found, the slaves set free, the sinners redeemed, the condemned pardoned, the enemies reconciled, the traitors forgiven and restored to citizenship and the favor of the King. This package we call salvation, and it is all a byproduct of the fact that for us men—and our salvation—One came down from Heaven to seek and to save that which was lost. We could say we are justified, adopted, regenerated, sanctified, and glorified; we could say we are saved; or we could say that the Shepherd has found the sheep that was lost, taken him up in His strong arms, and carried him back to the fold.

PRAYER: Father, may this truth be the cornerstone of all my thought: Thou didst see me a broken thing in this world's rubbish heap and saidst, "My own!" Amen.

Descendit
"Who ... Came Down"

"Who for us men and our salvation *came down*." We have been forced to concoct whole lexicons of words to try to describe this stooping. We speak of the humiliation of Christ, His condescension, His grace, His unmerited favor, His sacrifice, His adopting the form of a servant, His poverty, His suffering, His anguish. He was despised and rejected of men; He came unto His own and His own received Him not. His appearance was marred more than any man's; He was betrayed and condemned and died the death of a criminal. We've tried technical terms like *kenosis*, from the Greek word for the emptying of Phil. 1:7. We have stood in open-mouthed horror as His cry of dereliction echoes in our consciences: *"Eloi, Eloi, lama sabachthani"* (Mat. 27:46). We have a whole vocabulary of words that try to bring us into contact with the reality of this coming down. And while each of them says something and each of them is valuable, not all of them together can even begin to say it at all.

To comprehend the full depths of this descending, we would have to have some experience first of the heights from which it began. We would have to be able to imagine what God was like in His self-sufficient splendor before the worlds were made, when there was no space-time continuum in which anything could be located and He was simply All. We would have to know the dynamics of the inter-Trinitarian Love which was His life as He dwelt for untold ages (there being as yet no way to measure time) in a perfect, self-contained ecstasy of serenity and joy. We would then have to comprehend as part of that eternally abounding love and joy the impulse to creation so that His glorious life might be reflected by and shared with wholly unnecessary beings like ourselves. We would have to be able to glimpse that Heaven in which He dwells with His angels, beings themselves of unimaginable power and beauty who must nevertheless veil their faces before His supreme majesty. We would have to be able to pierce the clouds of glory around His throne where He ever dwells in unapproachable light.

Then from that unimaginable height we would have to begin our dizzying descent into the murky depths of the material world. To have entered even the unfallen creation would have been a stooping of inscrutably vast dimensions: to have that Mind used to the freedom of infinite intelligence with unlimited access to all of the created world suddenly cramped and encased in the narrow grave of a skull, to try to operate through the flickering neurons of a few paltry million nerve cells. How suffocating it must have seemed! To be limited to one place, one time at a time, subject to the rhythms and needs of the body; to be reduced to the information fed in through what must have seemed the dull and misty windows of the five senses: C. S. Lewis captures the idea, though not the real extent, of it by suggesting, "Imagine how you would like to become a slug."[12]

But the Son's descent was far deeper even than this. It was not the pure and beautiful world of His own creating that He would enter, but one marred, cursed, and corrupted by sin. Though His virginal conception was a sign that He himself was not infected by that corruption, He was surrounded by it, He was grieved by it, and He was burdened by it. That burden would eventually bow Him so low that He could no longer see the Face of His Heavenly Father, for He had become so completely identified with our sin that Scripture even says He *became* sin for us. Even the strength of omnipotence was tested by that trial: the mere contemplation of its approach made His body sweat as it were drops of blood.

Into these depths indeed we cannot peer very far. The Good News is that He came down precisely so that we would not have to.

Praise Him!

PRAYER: Father, Thy Holy Child showed us how Thy love looks in the likeness of sinful flesh. Enable us to have the same Mind of Christ, the layings down and takings up necessary to follow Him. Amen.

Descendit de Coelis
"He Came Down *from Heaven*"

It was fashionable in the Twentieth Century to patronize Christians of earlier times as naively mythological in their thinking. They supposedly believed in a three-storey universe, with Hell below, Heaven above, and earth in the middle. It might have been OK for Dante to think of Hell as actually located in the earth's core and Heaven on the other side of the glass sphere that holds the fixed stars, but now we know better. We can't really believe the way the people who wrote the New Testament and the creeds did anymore, so we have to "demythologize" those texts. Thus we get rid of nasty little inconveniences like literal heavens and hells, miracles, virgin births, and bodily resurrections, but still believe in the "spiritual essence" of the teaching of Jesus.

Oh, really?

Christianity contains some doctrines that are hard to believe; make no doubt about it. But what is *really* hard to believe is that the nonsense expressed above seemed so easy to believe for so long. If we are looking for naivety, we hardly need to go back into the deep past to find it. In fact, one could make a good case that there was a lot *less* of it abroad then. I don't recall running into an abundance of glass spheres in the Bible, which has the earth suspended on nothing (Job 26:7). Joseph was under no illusions about what to think when his fiancé turned up pregnant (Mat. 1:19). Jesus had a much more hard-nosed and realistic estimate of what is in the heart of man than any secular humanist I've ever met (Jn. 2:24–25, Mat. 15:19). And to suggest that Dante, the greatest *allegorist* of all time, for goodness' sake, couldn't tell the difference between a symbolic representation and the reality it represents? Well ....

The Bible is neither naive nor is it abstract. It deals with spiritual reality *as it manifests itself to the senses* and quite frankly tells us that we have not yet imagined what the other world is really like (1 Cor. 2:9). But that does not mean that the authorized manifestations are either untrue or dispensable. If the disciples saw Jesus be taken up from them and disappear into a cloud when He returned to the Father (Acts 1:9), then that is what they saw. And if God presented the withdrawal of Christ from this world to their senses in that fashion—and told them to look for His return in like fashion—I for one am willing to believe He had a good reason for it.

So, the entry of the Divine Spirit into the material world is represented thus: "He came down from Heaven." He came to us, in other words, from a kind of existence that was as exalted as the limitless sky, glorious as the sun rising in triumph over the darkness, pure as the light of the morning star, eternal as the predictable paths of the planets in contradistinction to the decay, corruption, and death to which everything in this world is subject. He came down from Heaven. Like a king who comes down from his throne, down from the high table on the dais to serve with the scullery maids in the kitchen, He came down. (Perhaps what we *really* need to do for modern readers is to *re*mythologize the Bible!) He came down from Heaven, says the Creed; and if you can think of a better way to say it, you will do something that has not been accomplished by all the sages of Earth for two millennia.

Hell is not the less real for not being a hole in the ground—but it is as low as you can get. Heaven is not the less real for not being a planet orbiting some distant star—but to leave it is to come *down* in the geography of the spirit. And our Middle Earth *is* located between the two, for in spite of all its beauty it is a place where we cannot stay. It has many goodly inns, but no permanent dwellings, and every road that goes by the inns terminates ultimately on one of the other two kingdoms: the Dungeon or the Dais.

On that Dais around the High Table the knights of the High King are gathered. There believers in Christ are already represented by the One who came down from Heaven so that they might arise. And when they gather around His Table here on earth, they both remember His coming down and anticipate the day when they will be with Him in His Kingdom—and the real Feast begins.

PRAYER: Father, keep our thoughts alert on that Road most arduous and less traveled, thankful for rests along the way, and grateful for the company of those who ever point us to that place from which He descended in order to return, and not alone. Amen.

Et Incarnatus Est
"And was incarnate ..."

Incarnation is one of those words that we have used so often we have forgotten what it means. We have taken what was once the most shockingly concrete word ever uttered and rendered it down into a powerless and completely unthreatening abstraction. To recapture its proper potency, though, all we have to do is remember the Spanish descendant of the original Latin root, which still retains its pristine precision: *carne,* as in *chili con.* What we confess in the Creed is that the eternal, holy Son of God came down from Heaven and was made meat.

The extent to which this translation seems irreverent is an index of how successfully Gnosticism has infiltrated our minds, which betray the hollowness of their formal orthodoxy when they are confronted with the reality of what it means to worship an incarnate God. The Gnostics were a profoundly spiritual people, so much so that any entanglement in the material world seemed problematic for them. That is precisely why their influence has ever been deadly to true Christian spirituality, which is the adoration of a Spirit who is in love with the physical world. As C. S. Lewis so pertinently said, "God likes matter. He invented it."[13]

To be squeamish about the union of godhood with flesh is to betray a lack of sympathy with the God who made the world and called it good. It is to refuse the Spirit who performed the first marriage and inspired the Song of Solomon. And it is to reject the Son who came down from Heaven and joined Himself to a body of flesh and bone, so strong was His identification with the creatures He had made and lost and come to find again. Hence the Gnostics were condemned by Apostles and Councils as anathema: They denied that Jesus had come in the flesh. But, kicked out the front door of the Church though they were, they have been sneaking in the back door ever since.

These backdoor Gnostics show themselves in the tendency to equate sin with pleasure, and righteousness with the length of the list of pleasures we are willing to abstain from. Their presence is felt in the popular soteriology that focuses on "going to Heaven" as the real end of salvation, forgetting that Heaven is for us an unnatural "intermediate state" and that our biblical destiny is to glorify God in resurrected *bodies* on a renewed *earth*. Their influence is seen in the general lack of serious Evangelical involvement in the production or consumption of the arts, except for tacky and sentimental figurines, paintings with clumsily edifying messages emblazoned across them, or whatever can be justified on pragmatic evangelistic grounds. Their hand is evident in the blasphemous Sunday School portraiture that makes Jesus look like an effeminate will-o-the-wisp who would likely be blown into oblivion by the slightest breath of fresh air, should one be so daring as to intrude itself on His otherworldly presence.

No. We worship as God a man who worked with His hands in a carpenter's shop before the invention of power tools, whose best friends were fishermen, who made for a friend's wedding a batch of wine that got the attention of the connoisseurs even though most of the guests were already too drunk to appreciate it, who told stories about baking and gardening and herding sheep. He was a craftsman before He was a preacher, and the greatest artist of all time before He was a man, using the periodic table as His palette and space and time for His canvas. Those who misunderstood Him accused Him of gluttony, but not asceticism, the latter charge being too unimaginable to those who knew Him to be worth trying. He was the most truly spiritual man who ever lived, but "spiritual," as the adjective is used too often today, is the last word His contemporaries would have thought of applying to Him.

Well, if His followers are supposed to be like Him, then their religion will be the one that supremely affirms the value of the material world. They will consider no notion of spirituality to be complete that is not incarnate in holy flesh. And they will know with Gerard Manley Hopkins that "Meadow down is not distressed for a rainbow footing it, nor [we] for [our] bones risen."[14]

PRAYER: Father, sacrifices and offerings were not enough; a Body Thou didst prepare for Him. May His Spirit so rule my body that I, like Him, may prove Thy will as that only which is good and acceptable and perfect. Amen.

De Spiritu Sancto
"By the Holy Spirit ..."

"The Holy Ghost shall come upon thee," said Gabriel to Mary, "and the power of the Highest shall overshadow thee; therefore also that holy thing which shall be born to thee shall be called the Son of God" (Lk. 1:35). His words undoubtedly resonated in the Virgin's mind with the richness of powerful Old-Testament associations: the Spirit brooding over the surface of the waters to plant order and eventually life in the as-yet unformed womb of the earth; the Shekinah Glory settling like a cloud on the Tabernacle as a sign that Yahweh was resident there, personally present with His people. It was entirely appropriate that the Spirit who elicited life from the barren belly of Chaos should introduce the divine Life into the fertile womb of Mary, which as a result of that act would become for the next nine months quite literally the Holy of Holies; for from the Temple in Jerusalem the *Shekinah* had long departed.

The incarnate Son was the point of contact between the infinite God of spirit and the finite world of matter; the Holy Spirit was the line of communication between the human experience of the Son and the divine power and wisdom of the Father. It was not through the direct exercise of His own divine prerogatives but through reliance on the power of the Spirit that Jesus performed His mighty acts, as numerous passages imply (compare, for example, Lk. 1:35, 3:22, 4:18, Jn. 5:30). Thus, our High Priest entered fully into the life of our humanity, being tempted truly as we are, yet without sin. Though still possessed of His divine nature, our Savior held nothing back in his full identification with us, depending on the enabling of the Holy Spirit for His own ability to walk with the Father even as we must. It was in this dependence that Jesus was perfect; in this dependence as in all things he is our perfect example; and it began with His very entry into the world of matter through the Virgin's womb.

How the Holy Spirit accomplished the union of the Second Person of the Trinity with a human ovum is probably a mystery forever inaccessible to our finite minds. The method is not revealed, perhaps not revealable; but the Maker of the miracle is made known to us, and so is its meaning. As a result of the Holy Spirit's overshadowing Mary, Jesus is *Immanuel,* God with us:

The seed had slept some fourteen years, but now
There was more than silent darkness: something new,
A gentle motion, growing warmth. Somehow
The tiny cell knew what it had to do:
Glide on, and be receptive to its fate,
Either a greater change or death. The girl
Felt nothing whatsoever when the weight
That counterpoises all the blazing swirl
Of suns we call the universe was pressed
To needle concentration down and driven
Into her belly. She could not have guessed
The power of the Gift so softly given;
The egg would never be the same again.
It would have been annihilated by
The impact if the same Force had not been
Within, sustaining. Men who watched the sky
Were startled by a star they did not know;
The demons trembled, and did not know why;
In Mary's womb, the Seed began to grow.

D.T.W

PRAYER: Father, may Thy Spirit make us teachable toward what was true for Him and must be true for us: obedience is learning new ways of being emptied in order to be filled, of descending in order to ascend, of being buried in order to rise again. Amen.

Ex Maria
"Of the Virgin Mary"

The mother of Jesus was a young Jewish girl probably in her mid teens, betrothed but not yet married when she was visited by the angel. She apparently came from a family of humble circumstances despite its proud Davidic heritage. She was probably illiterate, since only boys would have been sent to synagogue school; but she had absorbed the spirit as well as the diction of the Old Testament scriptures through a rich oral culture, as she showed when she spontaneously composed that beautiful hymn, the *Magnificat*. But what is truly remarkable was her faith in God and devotion to His purposes for her people. For the sake of Messiah's coming, she agreed to become an unwed mother in a time and place where that stigma was still unforgivable.

The road she was asked to walk was a bitter one indeed. She had to see the pain of betrayal in Joseph's eyes when he discovered her condition. And though in an act of magnanimous kindness he decided not to shame her publicly, there must have been a look of betrayal in her own eyes as well when he turned and walked away. The conversations she had with her parents about that time are mercifully unrecorded. And then the angel talked Joseph into coming back, and that was a blessing. But she had to find it in her heart to forgive him for needing an angel's word for her innocence. Why couldn't he have just believed *her*? She must have known those feelings were unreasonable, but that knowledge would have done little to soften her own inner struggle.

Then there was the little problem of how to raise the Son of God. She must have, from the moment he got out of swaddling clothes, had the sinking feeling that she was in over her head. She probably soon learned not to say, "That's my son—the Messiah." And whether keeping it in or catching the whispers and the knowing looks behind her back was worse would be difficult to tell. Then there was that incident at the Temple after his Bar Mitzvah, when, once again, she misread Him completely, couldn't get the fact that he had to be about His Father's business (and He didn't mean carpentry), lost her temper, and ended up feeling helpless and utterly wretched. She'd overstepped the bounds again at the wedding in Cana and got those sharp words and that sharp look from Him, though he'd gone ahead and made the wine anyway. Then when, supposedly grown up, He'd started His ministry, He *wouldn't* take proper care of Himself, not getting enough sleep or even taking time for a decent meal. What's a mother to do? She had come with His brothers to try to talk some sense into Him, and *that* had been a total disaster in which He'd practically repudiated her in public. Was that any way for the Messiah of Israel to act?

It might have been worth it if He'd actually *done* anything. But what real good did all his preaching and healing do? What difference did it really make? Practical, dependable James had taken over the carpenter's shop when Joseph died, even though it was the oldest son's place to do so, and everybody understood, or said they did. And did Jesus ever visit or take any notice of their problems at home? Only once, and then it would have been better if He hadn't. He'd gone out of His way to insult the congregation in the synagogue. These people were their *neighbors,* for goodness' sake. But did Jesus think about that?

And then there would be the unspeakable horror of the Cross—watching her little boy take those spikes and seeing His body distorted in agony and wanting desperately to turn away but being unable to. All this had to take place before the Resurrection and finally real understanding and acceptance and joy ineffable. If she had known it all at the outset, would she have said yes? She must have wondered, shuddered at the realization that she might *not* have, and finally been glad for her youthful naivety at the Annunciation. Had it all been worth it? Yes. But that was not a "yes" that could come easily or cheaply.

The sentimentality that makes Mary the Mediatrix, the Queen of Heaven, an active participant in our redemption, an almost equal partner with her Son, and a contributor to the atonement of anything more than the willingness to be God's vessel, is theologically misconceived but psychologically realistic and devotionally understandable. What she paid was, in a sense, a necessary part of the Price. So when Jesus pointed to His disciples and said, "Behold my mother and my brothers," He might just as well have said, "If any man will come after me, let him deny himself, take up his cross daily, and follow me."

PRAYER: Father, may we, with that company for whom He thought the City with foundations worth preparing, heed His mother who still tells us through Thy Word, "Do whatever He says." Amen.

Ex Maria Virgine
"Of the *Virgin* Mary"

The virgin birth has become one of the great shibboleths of the Christian faith, dividing those who take seriously the idea that Christianity is a religion having to do with the intervention of an unapologetically supernatural *God* in human history from those who, for some unaccountable reason, wish to retain the name of Christian while disbelieving that Jesus was anything worth believing in. Sages, ethical teachers, and martyrs we already have in abundance—and some quite good ones, too. We don't need another one. But a Savior ... well, that's a different story.

Scripture is quite explicit that Mary was a virgin when Jesus was conceived and stayed one until after he was born. (It also implies that once He *was* born, she and Joseph enjoyed a perfectly normal—and fruitful—marriage, giving Jesus a number of half brothers including James, who was not one of the Twelve Disciples but who became a leader in the early Church.) And it implies that this miraculous conception is related to His role as Savior. Yet it is not entirely clear about *how* they are related. And therein lies some potential for confusion.

A common assumption is that the virginal conception of Christ was a prerequisite of His sinlessness, breaking the link with Adam that gives us our sinful natures. There is some truth here, but we must be careful how we understand it. For it would be difficult to prove biblically or scientifically that sin is transmitted through the father's chromosomes. If sin were transmitted genetically, Jesus would have picked it up quite as easily from Mary, virgin though she was. Indeed, the problem inherent in this kind of thinking has caused Roman Catholic theologians to have to keep pushing the miraculous break back further, creating the notion of the immaculate conception of Mary. But once we start this process, where do we stop? There seems no logical place until we get all the way back to Adam and Eve themselves.

Sin is not transmitted genetically but spiritually along the lines of fealty. We are all sinners, but not because we are physically descended from Adam. We are sinners because Adam chose disobedience as the Head of the human race—a decision that counted for all his offspring, and one we all ratify personally and individually as soon as we are able. That is what it means to be "in Adam." Jesus was not represented by Adam's decision; He was not under Adam's authority, but was a Head in His own right, a new beginning for the human race. He was the "second Adam," an alternative Head, and so the whole human race is given as it were an opportunity to transfer its allegiance. Believers then are righteous because Jesus chose obedience as the Head of redeemed and restored humanity—a decision that counts for all His disciples and which they all ratify personally as He makes them able. That is what it means to be "in Christ."

Whether Joseph could have been involved in the production of Jesus' human nature is something we simply don't know. But we do know that the virginal conception of Jesus functions perfectly as a *sign* that calls attention to the nature of His relationship to us. The line of descent from Adam was broken to show that the authority of Adam's decision had been broken; the old line was broken to show that a fresh start for the human race was possible. That is, Jesus was not sinless because He lacked Joseph's chromosomes; rather, Joseph was bypassed in the creation of Jesus' human nature to show that a change of dynasty was taking place, with a new King who would make different commitments being offered as an alternative to Adam. He was not sinless because He was born of a virgin; He was born of a virgin to highlight the new identity and role, the new relationship to the rest of the human line, that made his sinlessness both possible and relevant

The end result of all this is that the baby born to that virgin was a person who could become our Redeemer indeed. He is Immanuel, God with us; He is Jeshua, Yahweh saves; and He is the Son of Man, the new Adam, Head, Leader, Representative, King—everything to us that our first progenitor ought to have been. And all that is what we confess when we say that He was born of the virgin Mary.

PRAYER: Father, to show us that we, too, must be born, not of the will of man nor of the will of the flesh, Thou didst send Him born apart from these, born of Thy directive to the body of the mother of our Lord. May Thy directive through Him to us quicken His life within us. Amen.

Et Homo Factus Est
"And was Made Man"

Several times in the course of the Creed a flight of soaring affirmations comes to rest, banking in a graceful curve toward a position that could be called a bottom line. Such is the case here, as for us men—and for our salvation—the eternally divine Son came down from Heaven—was incarnate by the Holy Spirit—of the virgin Mary—*and was made man.* We have rung the changes on the paradoxes of it already: The One whose name was above every name became a little lower than the angels; the Almighty became helpless; the Omniscient One became ignorant; and the Holy One was even prepared to become sin for us.

Only two thousand years worth of familiarity could have dulled our sensibilities to the shocking nature of what we claim. We worship as God a first-century Jewish carpenter who abandoned his trade to become an itinerant preacher. He hung out with disreputable characters, liked a good party, and had to relieve himself when it was over. He managed to get himself lynched for being politically incorrect. His followers chickened out and deserted him, and had it not been for the intervention of a closet sympathizer his lifeless body would have been dumped into a common grave. And, oh yes—He also spoke like no man ever spoke, bossed around wind, waves, and demons, made the blind see, the lame walk, the dead live, and, perhaps even more miraculously, the living glad to be alive. And He came back from death Himself, transforming his cowardly disciples into a band of radicals that turned the world upside down. The world has seen lots of gods and lots of men, but only this One goes near to convincing us that He was somehow both at the same time.

His disciples were normal, ordinary people like us who found themselves caught up in something bigger than they knew how to handle. Far from being capable through their literary skill of transforming a mere man into something superhuman, they give the impression of just holding on for dear life and being carried along for the ride. And a wild ride it was, too, for it was their Master's very obvious and inescapable humanity that made His equally inescapable deity all the more astonishing.

They never did explain it, but they spent the rest of their lives trying to proclaim it, define it, and apply it, because they could not deny that they had experienced it: God was in Christ reconciling the world to Himself. The Nicene Fathers continued the process of proclamation and definition, and we continue to believe and apply what they handed down to us. We *still* can't explain it, but those who have known the Lord can't get around it either: The eternal Son of God, from the bosom of the Father, was made man. And we beheld His glory, as of the only begotten of the Father, full of grace and truth. Fully God and fully man, compromising neither nature, uniting both in one Person, so there is one God and one Mediator between God and man, the man Christ Jesus.

Ecce Homo, Pilate challenged us, "Behold the Man!" And he who has seen Him has seen the Father. Hence we know neither God nor man, neither the Father nor ourselves, until we know Him. And we *can* know Him precisely because He became one of us—our Representative, no less, the new Adam.

He was made man. And we can therefore become the children of God.

PRAYER: Father, we asked Thee, "What is man?" and "What is man that thou art mindful of Him?" And in answer Thou didst send us Him. Make us true Man in Him, letting that Mind which was first in Christ be also in us. Amen.

Crucifixus
"He was Crucified"

The Son came down for us and for our salvation. He entered the world through the womb of a virgin to highlight the fact that he was a fresh start for the human race, not implicated in Adam's rebellion. But how did His coming actually eventuate in salvation for us?

The Creed says nothing at all about Jesus' miraculous healings, his incomparable teaching, or his supreme moral example. And this should not seem strange. If the Gospels were as short as the Christological section of the Credo, yet retained their original proportions, they would skip to the crucifixion almost as quickly. Why? Because as important as those other things were, they were not the essence of what he did *for us and for our salvation*.

Not that they were irrelevant to it. The sacrificial victim had to be an unblemished male from the flock. Jesus acting as our perfect moral example, in other words, was not so much in itself what saved us; it was rather to establish his qualifications for the job. The job was to be what John the Baptist called him: the Lamb of God who taketh away the sins of the world. For apart from the shedding of blood there is no remission for sins. Therefore each one of the Gospel accounts, by its structure, its diction, and the very amount of space dedicated to Passion Week, focuses inexorably right on that very same climax of Jesus' ministry to which the Creed so quickly cuts: *Crucifixus*.

For a long time in the modern world it was fashionable to consider this version of the significance of Jesus, with its insistent focus on his Blood, to be primitive, crude, and barbaric. Primitive it certainly is. But to use the other two adjectives is simply to confess that we take sin much less seriously than the apostles—or our Lord himself—did. And that is to advertise, not our advancement, so much as our extreme superficiality compared with them. It is to cheapen God's justice, and hence, ironically, also his goodness and his mercy. But there was nothing cheap about the death of Christ.

Nothing less than an innocent death could atone for sin. And this death—public, humiliating, and exquisitely cruel—was was no doubt chosen by the Father as the most eloquent way of getting the point across: "*This* is what I think of sin." And, by taking the punishment on himself, he also said, "This is what I think of *you*": for God commendeth his love for us in this, that while we were yet sinners, Christ died for us.

Crucifixion was indeed one of the cruelest deaths ever devised by our insatiably cruel race. But let the Centurion in charge tell it in his own words, as it were:

> No question but it was a dirty job.
> The scourging by itself was bad enough;
> To drive the spikes, though, really takes a tough
> And calloused character. The women sob,
> The victim screams, and even as the mob
> Cries out for more, men wince. The really rough
> Part comes when all four soldiers huff and puff
> To raise upright the heavy wooden stob,
>
> For then the man's own weight begins to work:
> The tendons crack, the flesh begins to tear—
> And when he thinks it's more than he can bear,
> They drop him in the socket with a jerk.
> And after we did that, he said (it's true!),
> "Forgive them, for they know not what they do."

D.T.W.

And the Lord has laid on him the iniquity of us all.

PRAYER: Father, it pleased Thee to crush Him. Was the pouring out of His soul to death acceptable to Thee? Is this the satisfaction for Thee, that, by this death, many are justified and many made righteous? Father, grant that my inner vision may be filled with the sight of this self-immolating Love and so be part of what made the dying worth it to Him and Thee. Amen.

Etiam pro nobis
"Also for Us"

He was crucified also *for us*. When he said, "Father, forgive them," in other words, he was talking about you and me, not just the Roman squadron or the mocking bystanders who happened to be there at the time. Nor was he talking of the human race as an abstract collective. It was a consummately personal act.

The Son, we have already read, was incarnate for us, but that is not all. He was also *crucified* most specifically for us: on our behalf, for our benefit, in our place. This means that the crucifixion was not just an accident of history, whether the execution of an annoying rabble-rouser or the martyrdom of a pious saint. It had to do with our sins, our guilt, the death we should have died. If it were not for us, in other words, this blackest moment of human history need never have happened. It is because of us that the best man who ever lived was nailed to a stake of wood. I belabor the point lest in attempting to escape our responsibility for this horror we also escape its relevance for our lives: he was crucified for us.

Yet, though every man, woman, and child who has ever sinned is responsible for the Cross, we could not have brought Christ there alone. It was in the Father's plan for him from before the foundations of the world: for God so loved the world that he gave his only begotten Son that whosoever believeth in him should not perish but have eternal life.

The Cross is a figure of two lines meeting: God's hatred of sin and his love for us; our poverty and his provision; our misery and his mercy; our guilt and his forgiveness; our sin and his sacrifice. Most profoundly, it is God's own justice and his grace which meet to form this fulcrum on which the whole world hangs. The necessity that He uphold the standards of righteousness which flow from His own character and treat sin as it deserves intersects with His desire to find the lost sheep and bring it back to the fold.

And this intersection forms the crosshair that centers all of history on the heart of his Son.

For he died for us. Therefore, the patron saint of all the elect is Barabbas, who, as he walked out of Jerusalem a free man, could have looked up to the hill Golgotha and seen Jesus hanging on the cross that had originally had *his* name on it. I wonder if he stopped to think about what he was seeing. Jesus on the cross meant for Barabbas. The Innocent punished so the guilty could go free. The Substitute dying so the condemned could live. Did Barabbas shudder as he caught sight of the cross he had expected to occupy bearing Another? Did he just shrug his shoulders and walk on? Could he possibly have realized that Jesus had made the exchange on purpose? Imagine his feelings if somehow that fact could have come home to him.

But we do not have to imagine it. All of us who through faith in Christ stand before God uncondemned stand in fact in Barabbas' sandals; we need only look up, and we ourselves are there. We too are in the crosshairs of history. We need only, in other words, take the Creed in our mouths with understanding: for he was crucified also for us.

PRAYER: Father, I am Thine, once pawned by sin but now purchased by His death, pulled from the world's dump in the act of His dying, enabled in the reversal of my self-worship by the giving up of Himself on the Cross. Let it be no longer I that live but let it be Christ living in me, true to the meaning of the "for" enacted there on that Cross. Amen.

Sub Pontio Pilato
"Under Pontius Pilate"

Jesus was not the only founder of a major religion who was a superb moral teacher; Moses and Confucius did that. He was not the only god who was said to have appeared in incarnate form; Vishnu did something like that. He was not even the only god who is said to have died for his people; Persephone in a sense did that. But he is, as Dorothy L. Sayers pointed out, the only God with a date in history.[15] Nobody knows when Krishna walked the earth as an avatar of Vishnu; nobody knows when Persephone first began her yearly sojourn in Hades. Hence, these events are located in a mythological time and space that makes them other than literal. But Jesus was crucified under Pontius Pilate.

It is not that mythological events do not have a real existence. Winter and summer, seedtime and harvest happen every year as Persephone continues to travel her predestined path. Her story tells us something about these events that is not quite captured by talk of the earth's inclined axis and circuit around the sun. It is a different kind of truth, compatible with, not contradictory to, the scientific account. One speaks to the analytical mind, the other to the synthetic imagination; one to the practical person, the other to the romantic. One gives us facts, the other feelings; one supplies numbers, the other nuance; one speaks of quantity, the other of quality. History tells us what springs, summers, winters, and falls have actually transpired: which ones were particularly cold or hot, wet or dry, which ones contained other events the race has not forgotten. Mythology tells us something not quite otherwise expressible about what it is like to live in a world in which time passes thus. It would be a poor human being indeed who did not realize a need for something of both in order fully to understand the phenomenon of the passing seasons.

But mythology and history, though they ought properly to be partners in the construction of our experience, almost always remain estranged. We normally get one kind of answer to our questions or the other. And we often run into people so fragmented that they can only deal with one kind or the other. Real integration at a deep level usually eludes us. But once it happened, right under our very noses: God was born as a Man and died to give life to his people, and he did it right slap in the middle of the Roman Empire. The man who signed the order for his execution would have been in our history books (in a much more minor role, granted—but there) even if it had never happened. Christ walked right onto the stage where Caesar was already standing, and they have been jockeying for position ever since. And there is no real question which one will be standing center stage when the curtain finally comes down.

As C. S. Lewis marveled in *Miracles* and elsewhere, Myth became Fact without losing the heartbreaking quality that stopped us in our tracks when we encountered it only as a story. Or, conversely, Fact was taken up into Myth without losing its hard-nosed objective reality.[16] The Cross was so real that you could have gotten a splinter in your finger from it if you had been standing there. And the Death that took place there has a meaning so deep and inexhaustible that it will haunt you like Demeter and Persephone, Cupid and Psyche, or Orpheus and Eurydice, and you will never sound it out. Indeed, when those stories have sunk into oblivion, we will still be gathered around the Throne, asking each other to tell this one again.

The stuff of mythology stepped out into plain old mundane history, not in some obscure corner of the world but at the height of the greatest empire man has ever put together. And it continues to shape our story to this day. For he was crucified under Pontius Pilate.

PRAYER: Father, He is Author and Finisher, but it is our story of which Thou hast made Him both. Our anniversaries, our memorials, our times and places, our events strung like beads onto strings too short, are the beachhead of His redemptive invasion. May He henceforth be Savior and Lord of my moments as well as my years, my inches as well as my miles. Amen.

Passus
"He Suffered"

"The hour has come," Jesus said in John 17:1. "Glorify thy son, that the son may glorify thee." The hour to which he referred was the hour of his impending death, a Death against which the Son of the living God needed to steel himself. As He gathered His thoughts in preparation for his coming ordeal, it was life, not death, that first came into focus: "This is life eternal, that they might know thee, the only true God, and Jesus Christ whom thou hast sent."

If life is knowing God, then death is ignorance of God. But "know" in biblical usage frequently means not so much information as relationship. It is in this sense that the Savior's definition of life must be read. Life is knowing God; death is ignorance of God. Life is fellowship with God; death, alienation from God. Life is friendship with God; death, enmity with God. Life is union with God; death, separation from God.

The essence of death is not then the cessation of bodily functions; that is merely a symptom of alienation from the source of life. So it has been since our sin first separated us from God in the Garden. For that reason, the wages of sin is death. Those who do not know the Father through faith in the Son—who have not received the forgiveness of sin Christ died to purchase—are literally dead even while they live (Eph. 2:1).

Jesus' body was wracked and torn by one of the most cruel forms of torture ever devised by our sick race. The arms were nailed to the cross-piece through the wrists. The legs were twisted around to the side, with the knees bent, and fastened with a single spike through the ankles. The position itself is very awkward, and the only way to relieve it is by pushing against those spikes. It sometimes took victims days of screaming agony to expire.

But it was not the prospect of such physical suffering that caused Jesus to sweat blood in Gethsemane. No matter what they did to his body, he could not *die* as long as he maintained contact with the Father. But he was on that cross to be identified with and thus punished for the sin of all mankind. And so complete was that identification that even his Heavenly Father had to turn away from him. Then was heard that terrible, universe-ripping Cry of Dereliction: *Eloi, Eloi, lama sabachthani*: "My God, My God, why has thou forsaken me?"

From that moment, Jesus was a dead man. Once that moment of ineffable spiritual and psychological agony had come, it was only a matter of time until the physical struggle too would end and the body on the cross be still. And whether it takes an hour or a century, the end result for people separated from God is always the same. Thus did Jesus die for us precisely that Death which is the wages of sin. And though the body, still subject to sin and death, will not be fully redeemed until the Resurrection, because of Jesus' death we can know God again and thus have not just the hope but the reality of, the essence of eternal life as Jesus himself defined it.

The professional executioners in charge certified that, in the only sense that had meaning for them, the Jewish preacher was indeed dead. A spear thrust into his side let out blood that had already separated into its constituent parts—a sure clinical sign that the victim was in fact deceased. Little did they know, walking corpses that they were themselves, how right they were. "Earth felt the wound," Milton says, when the first Adam sinned and died.[17] And now that wound was reopened, with darkness, earthquakes, the rending of rocks and tombs. But by his stripes, the prophet had said, are we healed.

PRAYER: Father, Death has been proud, for on the earth it ruled what once was Thy Paradise, what once had free access to the Tree of Life. We choose death who choose our own way; He chose not His own but Thy will, though it meant the terrible turning away of the Face which was Life to Him. There was He made the reversal of my eternal rejection by what is ultimately the Only Good; in His rejection I am embraced. Amen.

Et Sepultus Est
"And He was buried."

Jesus' tomb: the very phrase seems strange, a bizarre yoking of two words that ought not to belong together once you stop to think about it. It wasn't His in the first place, for one thing. Its availability for his burial was an act of charity on the part of Joseph of Arimathea, to keep the Master's body from being unceremoniously dumped into a common grave. And He was only there for parts of three days before abruptly leaving, never to return. Yet that brief sojourn has indissolubly linked Him forever with that cool, narrow aperture hollowed into the rock.

Burial is the final irony by which we vainly attempt to disguise the indignity of death. We flush the veins with chemicals and apply a cosmetic flush of life to the face. The Lord's generation wrapped the body in linen coated with pounds and pounds of spice. Then this artificially good-looking or smelling object is put away so that no one has to see the defeat of our exercises in futility. A certain body of politic worms eats away at our delusions, but their banquet is held in a fine and private place. As long as they are undisturbed, so are we. So the skull gets to grin into endless blackness, and nobody has to grin back—unless its name is Yorick, a fellow of infinite jest whose last laugh is that to his favor we must come.

Jesus was buried. He was not destined to stay buried, but His interment, brief though it was, helps us to nail down the reality of His death. He was so dead, so lifeless, that His friends—not the cowardly disciples, but the Marys and Martha, Joseph of Arimathea and Nicodemus—felt the necessity of going through with the normal futile motions. So they wrapped Him in spices, laid Him in the cold, cold ground, and rolled the massive stone into place across the opening. And Pilate—never one to presume upon the cowardice of Jewish rebels—got involved too, sealing the stone in place and authorizing a squadron of guards to camp in front of it.

Thus the finality of death was made, if it were possible, even more final. And it was all quite futile indeed—just not in the usual way.

Before anyone quite knew what had happened, the guard had been frightened away and paid hush money, the tomb was standing open and empty, and a few (no doubt unreliable) people were circulating stories about angels in shining garments who said that Jesus was alive. The linen and the spices were still there, but He was not. Where He was is a matter for another chapter. But the empty tomb still gapes at us, mouth wide with a Message that would be incomplete without that particular messenger. You can still visit it today, or one just like it (nobody knows for sure). But whether it be the actual spot or just a reminder of what it was like, it is there, hard as a rock with the reality that, however we explain what happened afterward, Jesus, the Lord of Life, was thoroughly dead and definitely *buried.*

At least for a while.

PRAYER: Father, it was to them their last loving act: to anoint and give back to the earth the body of Him they loved. Earth it came from and to earth it must return. He was made subject even to this. May my consciousness be dead enough to its own selfishness to want a burying, alive enough to Him to want a burying with Him. Amen.

Et Resurrexit
"And He was Raised"

The utter finality of Death is perhaps the most gut-wrenchingly intolerable yet inescapable reality of life. The fact that one will never—ever—see the face, hear the voice, or feel the touch of that loved one again in this life is perhaps the hardest fact we ever have to face. The imagination rebels against it with every knock on the door, every ringing of the phone. Yet Hades is the only god who never answers prayer. And the one exception he made came to nothing when Orpheus turned instinctively to keep Euridyce from falling only to see her fade back into the shadows at the very threshold of the sunlit world. The ache at the end of that myth is the inconsolable ache at the heart of our earthly existence. Vanity of vanities, all is vanity, saith the Preacher.

The disciples were not expecting Jesus to be an exception. They were consumed by defeat, despondency, and despair, expecting a Roman legion more than a resurrected Lord. His prophecies to the contrary apparently never registered until after the fact. So when it hit them, they must have gone from the pit of Hell to the pinnacle of Heaven in an instant. When they had connected his Words with his Appearances, watched him eat fish and break bread with his nail-scarred hands, and confessed him to be their Lord and their God, they were seized by a Joy that transformed not only their own lives but the whole world. This, they realized, changes everything. The unbreakable iron grip of Death had been shattered; they had seen it with their own eyes; and they were henceforth animated by a previously uncharacteristic courage that left them undaunted by all the terrors, tortures, or threats that man or devil could throw against them. Christ was risen! He was stronger than Death, and he was their Lord. Therefore, nothing could stop them now.

Never—not even at the crossing of the Red Sea—had the hand of God reached down more dramatically to demonstrate His interest in human affairs, to vindicate His Champion, and to bring salvation to His people. For in the blackness of the tomb, God had reached out his hand, and those cells, three days cold and lifeless, began to glow with energy and warmth once again. God had reached out his hand and that blood, three days dried and separated into its constituent parts, began to flow once again. God had reached out his hand and that heart, three days silent, inert, and dormant as a stone, began to beat again—so strongly that it burst the bands of Death asunder forever. And Jesus had laughed in the face of Death and walked out of his dominion, having plundered it of all the souls of the previously departed saints. So, though Death would continue to reap his harvest, the permanence of his hold on his victims had been broken forever. For Christ is the Firstfruits of them that sleep.

We have gotten so used to the idea that the spine-chilling impact of it is lost on us now. Jesus was dead; he is alive. Not just in some mystical spiritual sense but physically and literally, he is alive. Not just as a reanimated corpse, but with a body transformed by and pulsing with the Life that was his before the world was, he appeared to more than five hundred eyewitnesses. They understood why the Gospel is Good News. There is forgiveness in Christ; there is *life* in Christ. This changes everything. We may now look into the eye of the Last Enemy with defiance: "One short sleep past, / and Death shall be no more; Death, thou shalt die!"[18] For Christ is risen.

Christ is risen indeed!

PRAYER: Father, the last to be created in the old was the first to be created in the new: Man in the re-created body of the Son of Man. Through Him the whole creation awaits its re-making. Through Him, my own bones anticipate their quickening. Grant that to know Him and the power of His resurrection become increasingly the mark towards which I press. Amen.

Tertia Die
"He was raised on the third day."

Jesus was raised from the dead on the third day. Why did this seemingly insignificant fact make it all the way into the Creed? Even the shorter Apostle's Creed, which wastes no words at all, includes it. Isn't it enough that He was raised? Why is the day so important?

For one thing, it emphasizes for us once again the radical particularity of the Gospel. It was the third day because it was the third day—not the second or the fourth. It is one of those points at which one stubs one's toe against the stubborn factuality of the Christian faith. This is not a "spiritual" religion that worships an abstract Principle or tries to orient life to a series of eternal truths (though of course it involves quite a few truths that are nothing less than eternal and which will decidedly reorient one's life). There is rightly and legitimately a philosophy of the Christian faith, but that faith flows not from philosophical ideas but from historical acts. God *did* things that changed the world, and He did them right out in regular history, the kind that flows past us every day, the kind in which, if the Declaration of Independence was signed on July 4, 1776, it wasn't signed on the third or the fifth.

The central question of Old-Testament faith is, "Why is this day different from every other day?" The answer is that on this day God smote the Egyptians and passed over our Fathers and delivered them from slavery. The world was filled with dead Egyptians and freed Israelites as a result, and it still contains a People and a Book who give stubborn testimony to the fact that the Day of Passover indeed happened. Both still make a difference because that Day was different. Christians could ask the same question every Easter, indeed every Sunday. Why is this day different from every other day? Because on the third day God raised Jesus from the dead.

But why *this* day? Perhaps because the third day gave time for the reality of crucifixion and death to sink in. Passover—hmmm, what a coincidence—passed, and the ladies were forced to wait in an ecstasy of suspended agony for the holy Sabbath to end before they could indulge in the therapy of labor, caring for the body of their fallen Lord and friend as their culture dictated. When they finally got there they realized they had a problem—who would move the stone so they could get access to it? Somebody had already taken care of the stone, but finding the body was a different matter. It found them instead. Any earlier, or any later, the moment of maximum impact would have passed. God, the master story teller whose stories are ultimate reality, always did have a flair for the dramatic.

Or, more accurately, we should say that God has a flair for combining the dramatic with the mundane, for inserting the dramatic into the mundane in such a way as to render it anything but. That seemingly insignificant little ordinal number in the Creed captures both in intense concentration: stubborn mundane factuality; a mythic deed that changed and still changes everything. Why is this day different from every other day? Why, indeed! Christ was crucified, dead, and buried—and on the third day, God raised him from the dead.

PRAYER: Father, First Days were made for the beginning of a universe, and so the new heavens and earth had their First Day when He arose. And my First Day was the day He rolled away the burden entombing my heart. Grant that I walk always in the newness of Life I find waiting for me in Him. Amen.

Secundum Scripturas
"According to the Scriptures"

Christians believe that Jesus died and rose again, which is the wonder of all wonders in itself. But the wonder is enhanced by the fact that He did it "according to the Scriptures." This means not just that Scripture tells us about it but that Scripture predicted it. And more than predicting it, we can say that Scripture promised it. Christ did it, in other words, in fulfillment of the Father's intentions as promised to His people in His Word.

Christians affirm a God who reaches out, who makes commitments, communicates them, and keeps them. He has intentions toward us, declares them, and fulfills them. He is a God of covenant and of promise who makes good His word. Those words are recorded and preserved for us in the Bible, and they are confirmed by the Cross and the Empty Tomb.

The Bible's primary function is not therefore merely to convey information, though the information it conveys in the process of fulfilling its primary function is solid and reliable. Its primary function is not even to teach doctrine, though the doctrine it teaches in the process of fulfilling its primary function is important and true. Its primary function is to be the medium of a relationship between God and His people. It allows Him to command, to promise, to converse, to instruct, to encourage, to admonish, and to love. It allows us to receive all of that and respond to it in worship and service as we appropriate the inspired words of His early servants as our own. And central to all of these divine promises and human responses is the thread of redemption through His self-giving, culminating in the coming of Messiah.

God promised us that He, through the Seed of the Woman, would crush the head of the Serpent who had ruined us in Eden. He promised Abraham that through his seed all the nations of the world would be blessed. He promised Israel a prophet like Moses, a Child who would be a wonderful counselor, the mighty God, the everlasting Father, the Prince of Peace. He promised us a Suffering Servant through whose stripes we would be healed. This Servant would render Himself as a guilt offering, and *then*, amazingly, see His offspring and be assigned a portion with the great. He was announced by John the Baptist as the lamb of God who taketh away the sins of the world. He said Himself that He had come to give His life a ransom for many. But as Jonah was three days and nights in the belly of the whale, so He would be three days in the earth, and if you tore the temple down, He would raise it up again.

So when He was crucified, dead, and buried, and the third day He was raised from the dead, He did it precisely according to the Scriptures. Martin Luther said that every word in the Bible is about Christ only everywhere. Strictly this is an exaggeration, but it is an exaggeration that makes a valid point. St. Paul said that the church is built on the foundation of the prophets and apostles, Christ being the chief cornerstone (Eph. 2:20). In other words, the church is only rightly built when it is based on the Bible in such a way that both Testaments are seen to point to Christ. In other words, He was raised the third day according to the Scriptures.

Jesus said that not one jot or tittle could pass away until all was fulfilled. That is the kind of book the Bible is. We can hold in our hands a miracle as great as any it records. And we believe them all because of the one that happened on the third day, according to the Scriptures.

PRAYER: Father, in Thy Book we have been given Spirit fleshed in letter. Let there be perfect unity between the letter-fleshed Spirit of Thy Scripture and the heart-fleshed spirit directing my thoughts, words, and deeds. Let Him quickly subdue all contention within me against Himself. Amen.

Et Ascendit
"And He Ascended"

The greatest story of magnanimous stooping ever told comes full circle with the steepest and most dizzying ascent ever attempted. Having descended from the glory He had with the Father before the world was, Christ returned in triumph to reassume His rightful place at the right hand of Power on high. From an unimaginable altitude to a dungeon-like depth and back again: if we could imagine the transit between such extremes—if we could have followed the Savior beyond the cloud that interrupted our view of His ascent from our world of death and darkness to that Heaven of splendor and unapproachable light—it would surely have afflicted us with terminal vertigo. For having been crucified, dead, and buried, having been raised on the third day according to the Scriptures, He ascended into Heaven.

The meaning of this ascent arises from the stooping it rounds off and reverses. He had first come down: The Crown Prince had descended from the dais to serve with the scullery maids in the kitchen. Not counting equality with God a thing to be grasped, He took on the form of a servant and became obedient unto death, even the death of a Cross (Phil. 2:5–10). By this stooping the Son had brought to full expression the mystery that had lain hidden in the core of His Father's heart: the mystery of Grace. So pleased was His Father by this performance that He gave His Son a Name above every name, that at the Name of Jesus every knee in Heaven and earth shall bow, and exalted Him. Back from the kitchen He came to be given a seat at the very right hand of that Throne from which all of creation is ruled.

For Him, it was a return home in triumph; for us, it almost feels like abandonment. But in that feeling, we are as shortsighted as the baby that complains of being left in its crib while its mother walks over to the stove to test the temperature of its bottle. In at least three ways it was, as Christ said, better for us that He go away.

First, He now represents us before the throne of God, daily making intercession for us in His office as Mediator (I Tim. 2:5). Though His Father's ear has always been open to the prayer of faith (in anticipation, perhaps, of the Sacrifice to which His Son was committed before the foundations of the world), it is surely a comfort to know that God now sees us in the wholly acceptable form of His Son, our Advocate, who has immediate access to His Father's ear as well as His heart.

Second, because He functions now as our Representative, the Second Adam, the Head of restored humanity, it is our own human nature that in Him has been exalted, advanced to such great glory. In Him, we are admitted to the throne room of Heaven and seated in the position of highest honor. Christ is our Head, we His body. Therefore, where He is, there we are; in a sense, we can even say that *what* He is, that we are: sons and daughters of God, heirs of God and joint heirs with Christ. Because He is in Heaven for us, it is as if we ourselves are truly already there as well.

Finally, in anticipation of the next major section of the Creed, it was necessary that Christ return to Heaven in order that the Comforter might come, sent by Him and the Father. Christ, having permanently united Himself to our human nature, no longer functions as omnipresent: He has a literal human body, like ours though transformed by the Resurrection. How then can He be present in the lives of all His people, spread out over the surface of the earth in every tongue, tribe, and nation? He is present immediately in each of their hearts through His personal Agent and Representative, the Holy Spirit, who unites us to Him and to the Father until He returns. There is more to be said of this later. For now, it is enough that we recognize it as one of the benefits of our confession that He ascended into Heaven.

PRAYER: Father, He became both the "where" and the "way to" for us, the End and the Means. His Ascension tells us that we, too, in Him are on our way Home. Let my heart grow warm with the thought that each day brings me closer to where He is. Amen.

In Coelum
"Into Heaven"

When our Knight in shining armor had conquered sin and death and left us to return home in triumph, represent us before His Father's Throne, and send His Spirit to be His Deputy during His absence, the Creed says He ascended into Heaven. Of what this means we know very little. Imagery of Pearly Gates and Golden Streets is only imagery in the first place, and imagery technically of the New Jerusalem, not Heaven itself. Clouds served only to mark the limits of how far the Apostles' eyes could follow His ascent. Not very far. But no matter how far we might look—no matter how carefully we might analyze the wonderfully beautiful and intriguing pictures sent back by the Hubble Telescope—we still would not be able to locate the glint of His diadem shining out from some far-distant star cluster or nebula. So where did He go? What are we affirming here?

For ancient man, the Heavens were a realm of light and splendor that contrasted with the relative darkness of earth. They were, even more impressively, a region of permanence and predictability that contrasted with the relative fragility and fickleness of life on earth. The sun, stars, and planets were apparently eternal and completely dependable. They were always where they were supposed to be; you could navigate by them or plant your crops by them. But beneath the circle of the Moon, everything was subject to decay, and while the seasons were somewhat predictable, nothing was dependable. It is no wonder they were tempted to think of the heavenly bodies as divine.

The Hebrews were as impressed by the contrast as anyone, but they knew better than to think the heavenly bodies were anything more than fellow creatures. Other gods were made of wood and stone and carried about by human hands, but the Lord made the Heavens. They also knew better than to think that the Lord was physically or spatially located in the sky.

The earth could be called His footstool, but even the highest heaven could not contain Him, much less the temple Solomon had made. Nevertheless, it conveyed something important to their minds to associate Yahweh in a special way with the heavens. For His thoughts are as high above ours as the Heavens are above the earth, and it was natural to picture Him as looking down on mankind from Heaven, since, containing the earth as they do, the Heavens are obviously much larger as well as purer and older than earth. If we are to use language at all we must think in pictures, and the picture of God living in Heaven is a good one. The point is that the Hebrews knew full well that that is what it is.

The language of those ancient Hebrews made it into the Bible and was picked up by the Greeks and Greek-taught Romans who gave us the Creed. These Greeks were not any more naive about the relationship of the eternal Spirit to the physical creation than their Hebrew predecessors had been. But they had to deal with some hard historical facts handed down to them by the Apostles. After His resurrection, Jesus did not die again, nor did He simply disappear; He left this earthly existence to return to the Father and send the Holy Spirit until His return. And He did it in such a way that the Apostles would not mistake what was happening.

What they saw was His body leave the earth and get swallowed by a cloud. What happened to it after that is a bit unclear, but the angel stressed that He would return the same way He had left. The cloud basically saved the Apostles the trauma of trying to see the unpicturable, but they knew well enough what had happened. Jesus was with the Father, and if you need a concrete image to picture the whereness of that, saying it is in Heaven will do quite nicely. It is a realm of dimensions that dwarf our own frame of reference, of purity and splendor that we can only see from afar; and His return from it is as sure as the coming of the next summer solstice. In other words, He ascended into Heaven.

PRAYER: Father, Goodness is natural to the new self Thou art making of me in Christ, and Heaven is its natural environment. Help me to begin to exhibit ways of thinking and doing as one of Heaven's native citizens. Let my life demonstrate clearly that here I am a resident alien; there with Thee, I will be perfectly at home. Amen.

Sedet
"And Sitteth"

Having ascended into Heaven, Jesus now *sits* at the right hand of the Father. Sitting can refer to rest, to the fact that Christ's atoning work is complete; but He continues His mediatorial work, and so the great Sabbath Rest is not yet, for Him or for us. Sitting can also have reference to ownership: The owner of the House *sits* with his family and guests at the table; the servants stand. As Milton says, significantly, "They also serve who only *stand* and wait."[19] It can also refer to taking charge of or executing an office. The judge *sits* on the bench; the rest of the people in the room must all rise and can only be seated after he does so. Congress is said to be "in session" (which means "sitting") when it meets to conduct that nation's business. And the leader of a committee is referred to, in a significant metonymy, simply as "the chair." This is James Tiberius Kirk or Jean Luc Picard striding on to the bridge of the *Enterprise* and occupying that central Chair that seems to fit him so well. Everybody knows what sitting in that Chair means. Its occupant is at the center of the nerve center of the entire ship. That is the point, as Kirk tells Picard in *Star Trek: Generations*, from which he can "make a difference."

The Son, in other words, having triumphed over sin and death and proved Himself worthy, was given a name above every name and invited to share the Father's throne. In one sense He had always been there, had always been making a difference. What changes after His ascension is that it is the Son of Man who now occupies that seat. Human nature—our human nature—having been taken up into the Godhead in the Incarnation, has now been exalted to that greatest of heights. Sitting in the Captain's Chair is now One who has been touched by the feeling of our infirmities, who was tested in every point like as we are, yet without sin. Every attribute of God is united with every attribute of perfect humanity in the Person who sits there. There is no better leader to follow. So every member of the crew can know beyond a shadow of a doubt that the mission will be successful and the Captain will get us home.

Speaking of home, the permanent residence of a great family is known as its "seat." Its members may range far and wide, but they will always come back here: It is their base of operations. Their ancestors' sweat has watered its ground; their bodies lie in its crypt. It is home. So, too, the Son is completely at home at the Right Hand of Power, and it is not a position that He is going to give up. And because He is the Head of restored humanity, the Head of His body, the Church, then it is our home too if we are united to Him by faith.

Sitting is an image of rest, authority, and possession, but also of security and permanence. A person in a chair has sat down and settled in. He is much less likely to fall down or walk away than someone who is standing. So Jesus isn't going anywhere (until He returns for us). We always know where we can find Him: at His Father's side, making intercession for us, representing our interests, taking possession of the Family Seat in our behalf, preparing a place for us. If it were not so, He would have told us.

Rest; authority; ownership; stability: vested in Christ and therefore held for His disciples. All this at least is what it means to say that Christ is "sitting" at the right hand of the Father.

"At last the three companions turned away, and never again looking back they rode slowly homewards. ... Sam turned to Bywater, and so came back up the Hill, as day was ending once more. And he went on, and there was yellow light and fire within; and the evening meal was ready and he was expected. And Rose drew him in, and set him in his chair, and put little Elanor in his lap. He drew a deep breath. 'Well, I'm back,' he said."[20]

PRAYER: Father, Grant that the settled peace of Christ's seatedness by Thee be distilled into the scattered unruliness of my inner life, ordering my thoughts and emotions about Him, making His Glory and the Glory of His Kingdom the orienting point of all my desire. Amen.

Ad Dexteram Patris
"At the Right Hand of the Father"

The place from which Jesus came and to which He returned, the place where He belongs, the place where He sat down, and hence the place where we know we can find Him, is at the *right hand* of the Father. The right hand is the one that most people use for their most significant work. It holds the hammer, the sword, the brush, or the pen. And therefore the position at the right hand has always been the one of greatest honor. We refer to our most useful and indispensable servant as our "right hand man." The disciples foolishly wanted to know who would sit at Jesus' right hand (and His left) when He came into His kingdom. Well, that would be granted to those for whom it was reserved, and they weren't to be concerned with it now. But Jesus Himself had a place reserved at a right hand, and this one we do know. It is the right hand of God.

Because Jesus had humbled Himself, even to the point of death on a Cross, God has exalted Him, Paul tells us. In other words, the words we hope to hear on the last day, Jesus as our Representative has already heard: "Well done, thou good and faithful servant." In Him, those words are meant for us. And as we humble ourselves beneath His yoke, we too will be exalted and, hearing those same words, receiving that same crown of glory, will have the privilege of laying those crowns at His feet.

Sitting at the Father's right hand, Jesus displays the relationship He has had with the Father from before the world was, when He as the eternal Logos was with God and was God. The Father does nothing except through the Son—His right-hand man—and the Son's meat and drink is to do the will of the Father. In fact, He does nothing except what He sees the Father doing. The Father is greater than the Son—it is the Son who is the Father's right arm, not vice versa—but it is equally true to say that He and the Father are one. He is the Wisdom of God, the only One who can sit as His Counselor, the one in the perfect position next to the Throne always to have the Father's ear. And He constantly speaks into it an irresistible message of gracious intercession for His Chosen. For He is also the Power of God, God's strong right arm by which He redeems His people. And to them He is the Head of His Body, the Church, through Whose mediation they have immediate and unceasing access to the Throne at the right hand of which He sits.

This position of honor and favor, which the Son possesses as His birthright and which He also earned through His obedience, is bestowed on His people by Grace. He takes that Seat as our Head and our Representative. In Him, we are there. He is there for us. Therefore, we who deserve God's righteous judgment enjoy instead His favor: not just because Jesus died for us (though the importance of His death cannot be overemphasized), but because His death was accepted and He was raised and exalted and seated at God's right hand. That is why we may call His Father also *our* Father, our Father in Heaven. That is why the Holy Spirit, the Representative of our Representative, fills our hearts with confidence to enter the Holy Place and cry, "Abba, Father." And that is why we, like our Lord who came to reveal the Father, are sent forth with the same mission as Ambassadors of Christ to make disciples of all the nations.

When Evangelicals speak of the Christian life as a personal relationship with God through faith in His Son Jesus Christ, they speak an important truth. The Creed reminds us in these words that an important part of the basis and ground of that experience is the Session of Christ at the right hand of the Father. That seat is therefore the center of our world and the place to which we look for our redemption. And as the Creed continues, it reminds us that it is from that very place that even now our redemption draweth nigh.

PRAYER: Father, He loved righteousness and hated iniquity and therefore Thou didst anoint Him with the oil of gladness above His fellows, there at Thy right hand from which come pleasures for evermore. And there He invites me to participate in His Nature and Thine, loving what He loves, hating what He hates, being glad with the gladness He is in Himself. May my response be one of joyful haste. Amen.

Et Iterum
"And Again"

That the Son should ever have come down from Heaven and been made Man; that He should have lived among us a perfect life and taught us with authority, not as the scribes; that He should have died in our place a sacrificial death of atonement for sin; that He should have been raised in triumph from the grave, exalted to the highest part of Heaven, and seated at the right hand of the Father's throne to represent us there: All this, one would think, would have been enough to give our lives meaning and make it possible for us to live them. But then comes this next Word, laden with potentialities and making the blood rush with excitement: "Again." Again? After all this, what could the Son possibly do as an encore? The word appears, so there must be something, one last curtain call before the house lights come up for good.

Many things that God does are so good that they are worth doing again. There was morning and evening, the first day, and God saw that it was good. Millions of days later, He is still repeating the same pattern. Spring, summer, fall, winter: that too is a cycle worth repeating, and one that will be repeated as long as the world lasts. The animals in Eden brought forth after their kind, and there has been no need for an alteration of that pattern since. The Hero goes on an epic journey and, at great personal sacrifice, rescues the damsel in distress from the dragon; they ride off into the sunset and live happily ever after. It is a story we never get tired of hearing—for it is our Story, the one that tells us who we are.

But while God does things that are so good they are worth repeating, He is so creative that their recurrence is never repetitive. He keeps doing the same things, but never the same thing twice. Morning and evening are as old as creation and as new as a newborn babe: always the same, but never exactly the same. Why is this day different from all other days? Because it comes fresh from the hand of God. Every year, every generation is equally fresh and familiar. And we, His Subcreators, have made so many permutations to the Plot of the Story without essentially changing it that we can still feel the suspense, still feel the inevitable surprise, the joy of the happy ending, when the next wordsmith tells it anew.

So it is with the great Encore, the Sequel to the Gospel Story that is not just a sequel but the inevitable conclusion that flows from its original core of meaning. It is Jesus coming; Jesus coming *again*. Just the same, except different. All that was promised, indeed all that was won by His first coming, which to experience even in anticipatory form as the earnest of its future fulfillment makes life worth living, we will then have in full.

For while the just wrath of God was completely satisfied by the Cross, His love was not satisfied, not finished by a long shot. Christ has sent His Holy Spirit to be with us in His absence. But even with this He is not done. We are promised that this same Jesus will come again (Acts 1:11) in power and glory to judge the quick and the dead; that in that Return the dead will be raised incorruptible (I Cor. 15:52); that all that sin and death has taken from us will be restored as He reigns forever as King in a new Jerusalem. We no doubt know very little of what this all means. But we know we will be like Him when we see Him as He is—that one day we will see Him face to face (1 Cor. 13:12). And that is surely enough to tell us that finding out the rest of it will be well worth the wait.

PRAYER: Father, His stories all point to the "again" which He promised and for which we wait. Will He find faith which sees the return of the King, the netted fish, the fruitful field, the Bridegroom's coming as worth the wait? Grow that faith in me which sees the reality enough to watch and pray. Amen.

Et Iterum Venturus Est
"And He will Come Again"

That Jesus came is the best news ever shouted from the housetops. And there is only one other piece of intelligence that could rival it: the fact that He is coming again.

The two comings of Christ are a curious phenomenon in Scripture. The Old Testament never clearly distinguishes them. Indeed, from the Old Testament alone one would get the impression that the coming of Messiah to deliver His people and judge the world was to have been a simple and singular event. Jesus' heretical notion that the Davidic Messiah was the same Person as the Suffering Servant of Isaiah, and that His coming would involve two phases—now in suffering and humiliation, later in power and glory—was one of the reasons He was rejected by the Jews. To this day a standard Jewish argument is that Jesus could not have been the Messiah because the Messiah is supposed to bring peace on earth, and, well, just look around us.

The Christian response to this is that Jesus' resurrection establishes that He was the Messiah whether He fits our preconceived notions or not, and therefore we simply have to accept the One God sent us. While the Old Testament would not have allowed us to predict the two-phased nature of His coming, nothing about what actually happened contradicts its teaching. And its emphasis on the unity of that coming is by no means misplaced; it was just a more complex unity than we might have predicted. For example: is driving a nail one act or two? One can analyze it either way. One must raise the hammer, then strike the blow; but the twofold motion achieves one purpose. So it is with the coming of Christ: He came to give Himself a ransom for many, and He will return in power and glory to judge the quick and the dead. In the interim, the offer of salvation is extended to the Nations. And all of this achieves the unified purpose of God: to bring glory to His Son by the salvation of sinners.

So this same Jesus will come again. And it will be the same: personal and perceptible, objective and actual, visible and verifiable, predicted by prophecy, prayed for by His people, prepared by Providence, effected by the Almighty. But the two phases of God's coming to His people, His ultimate self-revelation, will also differ: as climax from crisis, completion from commencement, fulfillment from promise. And the differences are just as significant as the similarities. He came in meekness; He will return in majesty. He came in poverty; He will return in power. He came to the hay; He will return from the heights. He came in humiliation; He will return in honor. He came to glares of hatred; He will return with the glory of heaven. He came to be mocked; He will return to be marveled at. He came to be whipped; He will return to be worshiped. He came to be executed; He will return to be exalted. He came without prestige; He will return with all preeminence. Thus the two phases of His coming to us differ with respect to His person.

His return can also be compared to His first coming from the standpoint of His office. He came as a peasant; He will return as a potentate. He came as Servant; He will return as a Sovereign. He came to experience suffering; He will return to exercise sway. He came to the trial of a criminal; He will return with the triumph of a King. He came to be vanquished; He will return as the Victor. He came to be killed; He will return to be crowned as King of Kings and Lord of Lords.

We can also distinguish the two phases of His coming with respect to His work. He came to be judged; He will return as a Judge. In His coming He took on our nature: His return will transform our nature. His first coming brought atonement for sin; His second will be the end of sin. He came to bear punishment; He will return to bring peace. His first coming issued in the founding of the Church; His second will be the fulfillment of the Church. He came to win His bride; He will return to wed her, and they will live happily ever after.

It is simply the best news since the news that He has come: Jesus is coming again.

PRAYER: Father, the backward undoing of sinful humanity requires humiliation as the first step to glory and death as the doorway to life. Help me to hasten the glory of His return by willingly taking on my share of His body's sufferings yet to be filled up. Let His return be the joy set before me for which I make light of the sufferings of this present age. Amen.

Cum Gloria
"With Glory"

When Jesus comes back, it will be with great glory. The glory He had with the Father before the world was, which was veiled through most of His earthly ministry but revealed in flashes, as on the Mount of Transfiguration, will then be blazoned across the heavens for all the world to see. As the lightning shines even from the east unto the west, every eye will see, every knee will bow, and every tongue will confess that Jesus Christ is Lord, to the glory of God the Father. But what does this mean—what is this glory that will thus be revealed in the Son of Man? It is the majesty and splendor of God, before which the angels veil their faces. It is the glory that we fall short of in that all of us have sinned. But it is the glory that our Lord still possesses, and which he will share with His people as the capstone of their redemption, when they put on the morning star.

The English word *glory* translates the Greek *doxa,* which means radiance or splendor, hence that which catches the eye, hence fame, honor, renown. Jesus' face in Revelation shining like the sun, his robes flashing like lightning so that one could hardly look on Him, is the idea. The Hebrew word gets to the same end by a different route: *kabod* has as its root meaning weight or heaviness, hence that which abashes by its gravity, hence fame, honor, renown. When used with reference to God, it evokes the massive, almost oppressive impact of His presence. One thinks of Ransom's experience on Perelandra (from C. S. Lewis's Space Trilogy—the hero, Elwin Ransom, is experiencing God on a strange planet):

> Maleldil was not absent. That sense—so very welcome, yet never welcomed without the overcoming of a certain resistance—that sense of the Presence which he had once or twice before experienced on Perelandra, returned

> to him. The darkness was packed quite full. It seemed to press upon his trunk so that he could hardly use his lungs; it seemed to close in on his skull like a crown of intolerable weight so that for a space he could hardly think.[21]

The combination of the meanings, the connotations, the feelings evoked by both words comes close to the fullness of the biblical concept. In the year the king Uzziah died, Isaiah saw the Lord high and lifted up, with his train filling the Temple, which was smoking and shaking at His Presence and ringing with the voices of the cherubim crying "Holy, holy, holy." When the sky rings with the sound of Gabriel's trumpet, the heavens are rolled back like a scroll, and the Son of Man appears in His glory, all those unprotected by the Blood of the Lamb will cry out like Isaiah, "Woe is me, for I am undone; for I am a man of unclean lips." But it will be too late then for an angel to bring a coal from the altar to touch our lips. We will either have already confessed Christ as Lord and be able to welcome Him back with joy, or we will be crying out for the rocks to fall on us.

When Christ came the first time it was in humiliation; when He returns it will be in exaltation. When He came before, His deity was veiled in His humanity. When He returns, His divinity will be revealed through His humanity. God's glory is the awesome splendor of His majesty, power, holiness, and grace made manifest in the created world. And when our Lord returns, it will be made clear that, in this sense, the glory of God finds its ultimate definition, its most piercing revelation, and its everlasting focal point in Him. To Whom be glory forever and ever, amen.

PRAYER: Father, break through what my imagination is too ready to dismiss as special effects or explain away as commonplace natural phenomena with the reality of Thy Glory and His, His Glory and mine. Let the interests of His glory occupy my consciousness; let its dimensions shape my imagination. Let the details of my life be all for His glory. Amen.

Iudicare
"To Judge"

When Christ returns in power and glory, it will not be just a display of His divinity. He will have an active function to perform as well: to judge the quick and the dead. He did not come the first time to condemn, but to save (Jn. 3:17). But the Father has committed all judgment into His hands (Jn. 5:22), and when He returns it will be time for that judgment to be exercised.

Shall not the Judge of all the earth do right? (Gen. 18:25). Indeed He shall, and therefore He cannot wink at sin. As Romans 3:25–26 implies (cf. 2:4–5), in the light of God's justice, his forbearance of sin for thousands of years of human history requires an explanation. That is why the Cross of Christ was necessary: not just as an expression of the Father's love and grace, but as the vindication of His righteousness. Justice demands that sin receive its due, and because sin is high treason against our good and gracious King, the wages of sin is death. So why have all these traitors been allowed to live out their inexcusable lives? Why has God allowed the human race to continue in existence, spreading misery across the planet it is supposed to be dressing and keeping? Patience, forbearance, even love are not sufficient answers, for He is not a private person but the high King, responsible for maintaining justice and right in His realm. The answer is simply that no sin *has* gone unpunished. And the proof of this assertion is the Cross of Calvary.

Sin was judged at Calvary, finally and decisively. The word *propitiation* in Romans 3:25 means that the full measure of God's righteous wrath against sin, His holy displeasure with our rebellion, fell upon Christ there as our Representative. That is why God can in vs. 26 be simultaneously both just Himself and the justifier of the ungodly: simply forgetting about unpunished sin would not have been a just thing to do. The Cross allows

God's grace, His unmerited favor, and His justice both to find expression without compromise to either. That is the wonder of the atonement.

But this propitiation-based atonement applies only to believers. Those who have not believed are condemned already, while those who believe are justified, accepted by God as innocent because their full penalty has already been paid (Jn. 3:18, Rom. 3:24). All sin, in other words, will be judged, will receive its inevitable punishment. For those who have accepted Christ as Savior and Lord there is no condemnation (Rom. 8:1) because their sins have been judged already. For the rest, there remains the terrifying expectation of judgment (Heb. 10:27). And it is a terrible thing to fall into the hands of the living God (10:31).

Judgment is not our favorite doctrine, understandably so. But we do not fully understand either God or sin unless we realize that it is precisely a very good thing that sin be judged. Would we rather that God just turned a blind eye to our selfishness, our malice, our idolatry? The blood of all history's victims cries from the earth. But one need not shed literal blood to injure one's fellow man; we will give an account for every idle word. Sometimes words can cut more deeply than any sword. And because God does what is right, all those cries for justice will be heard. The books will be balanced, and the moral equilibrium of the universe, so skewed by our waywardness, will be restored.

More importantly, we cannot fully understand God's love unless we have reckoned with the demands of justice, the goodness and necessity of judgment. For it means that without the shedding of blood there is no remission of sin (Heb. 9:22). And that God commends his love for us in that while we were yet *sinners,* Christ died for us (Rom. 5:8). Whether at the Cross in His own person for us, or at His coming against us, Christ will judge. Blessed be He.

PRAYER: Father, I praise Thee for committing all judgement to Thy Son. I bless Thee for judging good what was first made through Him, for judging not good the loneliness of that first man, for judging and evicting what offended from Thy first Paradise. I praise Thee for the judgement which calls my sins by their true name and in so making me aware of my chains, makes me ready to be set free. Amen.

Vivos
"The Quick"

Jesus will come in power and glory to judge the quick and the dead. Those living at that time and those who have died: all of humanity will be subject to this judgment. The dead will be raised to face it, and the living will face it in the body they still have, but none will escape. We will all appear before our Maker to answer for the deeds done in the body. Woe to those who then must stand upon their own merits; happy are those who will be able to stand upon Christ's.

For the living, two implications of this coming judgment compel a response. First, it could happen at any time. And second, because it has not happened yet, it can still be prepared for. The fate of the dead, though not yet publicly pronounced, has already been fixed, and they can but await it. But the living can still do something about it, though they do not have forever to do so.

To confess that Jesus is returning to judge the quick is to remind ourselves that a chief purpose of this life is to prepare for the next. It is easy, caught up in it as we are, swept along by time from one moment to the next, faced by endless necessary tasks that demand our attention, and immersed in joys and sorrows that are none the less real for being temporal, to believe that this life is simply an end in itself. In fact it is such an end, for it is the arena in which we serve and glorify God and learn to know Him, and all these things are worth doing even here and now for their own sakes. But that is not all that it is. As nothing that is finite can exist on its own, so nothing that is temporal can have ultimate value except in relationship to the Eternal. And therefore part of what we are about in this world is the determination of what that relationship is going to be.

God's eternal purpose is to glorify His Son by saving sinners and incorporating them into Christ's Body, the Church. The Church will exist for all eternity as a holy Temple to the glory of Christ, made up of Believers as living stones. Thus will the wisdom and grace of God be made known to rulers and authorities in the heavenly places (Eph. 3:10). When time has run its course, all things will be summed up in Christ (Eph. 1:10). The Greek word for "summing up" in this verse could be accurately translated *thesis statement:* it refers to that part of a discourse in which all the parts are brought together, and the meaning and purpose of each in relation to the whole is revealed. In other words, Christ is the meaning of creation. All that has been made must find its meaning in relationship to Him. One purpose of judgment is to reveal what that relationship is. We will either find our meaning in Him or, having refused to relate to Him as Lord and Head, we will be cast into outer darkness. Hell is the trash can for all those paragraphs in the history of the universe which refuse to relate to the Thesis Statement.

The business of life then is to find the meaning of life. Even the pagan Socrates knew that the unexamined life is not worth living. And—what he did not know—that meaning is found only in Christ. In this life and in no other, in this world and in no other, we are choosing the meaning that our life will have for all eternity. Every choice, consciously or not, is but a part of that final Choice. And judgment simply reveals what it has been.

The gift of free will is a solemn thing, for God, having given it, honors His gift. We must choose what will be for us the meaning of life. At some point, that choice must be finalized. At death or at judgment, it is sealed, and there is no going back. For it is appointed unto men once to die, and after that, the judgment (Heb. 9:27). Since no one can predict the time of death any more than the day or hour of Christ's return, it behooves us to choose now and choose well. God's declaration by the Resurrection that Jesus Christ is Lord confronts us with that choice. And the promise of Christ's return to judge the living tells us that to be alive is precisely to be so confronted.

PRAYER: Father, grant that I may live with this habitual awareness, that every counted hair, every cell, every molecule of me exists of, by, through, and for Him and without Him, neither I nor anything else could exist. Let my will find its peace in His. Amen.

Et Mortuos
"And the Dead"

Jesus will return in power and glory to judge the living and the dead. That judgment will reveal the meaning they have chosen for their lives during the time that they lived. For the dead, the choice is already sealed, and they await its final revelation. In the meantime, Scripture suggests, they already anticipate it in their experience of the next life.

Even without the body, the soul maintains a kind of consciousness. The rich man in Jesus' parable carries on conversations in Hades (Lk. 16:19–31), the thief on the cross was told, "*This day* you will be with me in Paradise" (Lk. 23:43), and Paul tells believers that to be absent from the body is to be, not in a state of suspension, but "present with the Lord" (2 Cor. 5:8). At the moment of death, then, not only are our central life choices fixed for eternity, but we immediately enter into the experience of the life whose meaning—or lack of it—those choices have defined.

It seems rather hard to some that such a momentous destiny should be rendered unalterable at any moment, with no possibility of reprieve or of a second chance. But what would we have? If we want this present life to be significant, then significant it must be. And while we may not have known the full implications of each choice, we knew that we were choosing our own way rather than seriously searching for God's. We knew we were choosing the path of least resistance. We knew we were often rationalizing behavior that did not even meet our own standards. We knew we were choosing short-term satisfactions over long-term goods that were greater. We knew we were insisting on our own good even if it meant someone else's harm. We knew we had on occasion even intended that harm as our primary goal. So it is a bit disingenuous for us to suddenly wake up at the end of our lives and complain that we did not know we were choosing Hell.

Supposing we were offered a clear alternative: God will forgive you all those choices, wipe out the guilt they deserve because Christ paid their penalty on the Cross, and adopt you as His child to live with Him forever. And all you have to do to receive this Gift is make one choice: to admit you have been rebelling against Him, submit to Him—to let Him be God, in other words. Our natural inclination is to choose being our own God even at the price of exclusion from all that is Good, True, and Beautiful even then. That this Alternative is offered as a free gift to be received by faith is the Good News we call the Gospel. And by God's grace, some of us are enabled to accept it. Others are permitted to refuse.

The dead are those who are already experiencing, with a clarity not often permitted to the living, the fruits of those choices. Either in outer darkness or in the comfort of Christ's embrace, they wait for the signal that will summon them before the bar of judgment to resume the flesh, the fullness of personhood in which they made those choices, and in that flesh to hear their fate officially recorded and publicly pronounced before the universe. This is both for their sake, that there may be no question about the rightness and justice of God's decrees, and for the sake of principalities and powers in the heavenly places, who will marvel at the wisdom, the justice, and the grace of God (Eph. 3:10).

Christ will come to judge the living and the dead—and in both of those facts there is a message for the living. This life is not all. It is not the greatest good. And for that very reason, it is extremely precious. For here and nowhere else our acceptance or rejection of that Good will be decided for all eternity.

PRAYER: Father, Thou madest for our days a measure in order that, seeing their limits, we might incline our hearts to wisdom. Let the measure of my own days do their work in me, inclining my heart to Him Whom was made wisdom and righteousness for me. Amen.

Cuius Regni
"Whose Kingdom ..."

When Christ came the first time, the great slogan of His ministry was "Repent, for the Kingdom of Heaven is at hand!" The rightful Sovereign of Creation, in other words, who for eons had allowed the evil rebellion of demons against His rule to continue for purposes hardly to be understood by mortals, was about to reassert His dominion. This was a message of hope for humanity, hope for an end to the age-old struggle with meaninglessness, futility, and death precipitated by that rebellion. But it was also a sobering message of judgment, for humankind had become implicated in the rebellion through the Fall of its first Parents and its own waywardness ever since. Yet so gracious was the good Lord that the threat of judgment was turned right back into hope again by the word *repentance*, full of the promise of pardon. How deep that grace, how costly the forgiveness, how thorough the redemption thus planned and betokened: all this would be revealed by that first foray the King made into the territory held by His Foe. Some of it has been revealed in the pages of this exposition of the Creed already. And more is yet to come.

The Kingdom came in the person of the King. He landed to make good His claim on His ancestral domain, given to Him by His Father though long usurped by His Enemy. But this was not a King who would willingly lay waste a realm in order to reclaim it. There were the peasants—poor dupes of the Usurper who, though deserving His Majesty's wrath, were ones to whom He would rather show His compassion. And so began the most unorthodox campaign for the reconquest of a kingdom in the annals of military history. Not through strength but weakness; not through vengeance but mercy; not through killing but dying; not through wisdom but what looked to men like extreme folly was the Kingdom to be reestablished. And this was so that the people might have the opportunity to change sides freely, renew their allegiance to the true King, and thus become His loyal subjects rather than His prisoners of war. But let there be no mistake: His rule will be reestablished one way or another. In the meantime, we wait.

The Kingdom of God—the reign of Christ—exists already in the hearts of His loyal subjects. Already they enjoy the benefits of His benevolent rule: forgiveness for their former rebellion, hope for the future, a sense of purpose for the present as they work to extend that rule, the transformation of their character into the image of the King, goodly fellowship with their Lord and their fellow servants, the promise of eternal life. And—best of all—the promise that one day the King will return.

To prepare for that Day is the business of the King's subjects while they wait. They prepare their own hearts to meet Him. They recruit new members for the great Resistance Movement awaiting that return, the Church. And they try in the life of the Church to anticipate the reign of Peace and blessing that will be the experience of the whole world at last when He comes.

As C. S. Lewis put it in *Mere Christianity,* in words with special meaning given that World War II and the French Resistance were current events when they were written,

> Enemy-occupied territory—that is what this world is. Christianity is the story of how the rightful king has landed, you might say landed in disguise, and is calling us all to take part in a great campaign of sabotage. When you go to church, you are really listening in to the secret wireless from our friends.[22]

That is what it is like to be part of the Kingdom today. And one Day, the war will be over.

PRAYER: Father, "At hand," and "within you" He said of His Kingdom, and so we have found it. We are its citizens, our birth certificates issued from His throne. Make us both to stand tall and bow low in this knowledge, that we are the King's men and women. Amen.

Non Erit Finis
"And His Kingdom Shall Have no End"

The Kingdom which has begun but has not yet been consummated, which came with King Jesus and is coming with Him, will be like nothing we have ever experienced, for all our lives have been lived in the world cursed by the Fall. But we know that in it all that has been broken will be healed, that all our deepest aspirations will be fulfilled, and that humanity will finally live as it was intended to live. And we know that, once it has been set up—and it *has* been set up with the first coming of the King—it will go on forever. It will have no end. Christians debate whether a literal 1,000-year reign on this earth (the "millennium") will precede a final rebellion, final victory, and a new heavens and new earth. But pre-, post-, and a-millennialism are merely disputes over details of the King's itinerary. All true Christians agree on the final destination, and none of them think of it as impermanent.

At the time I first wrote this, my college had a president and an academic dean who had been with us for two decades but were reaching retirement age. This situation occasioned a great deal of speculation and discussion, and not a little anxiety about the future. Most of us would live to see a new administration. We were full of questions. Will it have the same vision of our institutional mission? Will it understand our way of doing things? Will it be competent? Will it have a leadership style we find it hard to adjust to? Things could get better; things could get worse. The one thing we were sure of is that they would not stay the same. We were right!

At the time of that writing, the United States was gearing up for its quadrennial presidential election year. There would be new faces in office at the end of the process. But there was already so much posturing, spin-doctoring, and tacking to the faintest shift of wind from the latest poll on both sides that everyone was very much afraid that nothing besides the faces would in fact change. And this meant that the change already in progress—the evolution toward a politics devoid of substance—would continue. And the end result of that must be that a change witnessed over and over in the history of our species will eventually be witnessed once again: the rise and fall of empires.

Alexander wept for lack of worlds to conquer and Caesar ruled over a domain like none had ever seen. But the glory that was Greece and the grandeur that was Rome survives only in fragmented form in museums, in the books of a few Dead White European Males, in the minds of their surviving readers, and in the Western Civ. courses which are themselves rapidly becoming museum pieces. This is a loss of cultural memory which may properly be mourned and ought properly to be resisted, but it has occurred and is occurring despite all we can do.

Everything that was won so gloriously at Agincourt by Henry V was lost by Henry VI. This is the summation of all human history. Our kingdoms never last because their kings never last. And even while those kings do live they are an insufficient foundation on which to build. But one Kingdom is coming—indeed has already begun—which will not share this fatal flaw with the rest. It rests on the strength of the Almighty, the justice of the Holy, the wisdom of the Omniscient, and the faithfulness of the Everlasting. Because its monarch is the One who made the world in the beginning and called it "good," He Himself being the Source of all goodness, all that was good in the earthly realms that have faded into dust will be preserved in it. And its duration will be coterminous with the Eternal One. Not only will all that has been lost be restored, but it will never be lost again. For He is the Son of the Ancient of Days, and His Kingdom will have no end.

PRAYER: Father, may the permanence of His Kingdom's reversal of our tortured planet's plight give us strong hope and encouragement through the dark days which yet remain. Amen.

III
THE SPIRIT

Et in Spiritum Sanctum
"And in the Holy Spirit"

Christians believe in God the Father almighty, Maker of heaven and earth, and in Jesus Christ, His only Son, our Lord. The Son is not the Father, yet is God; and yet God is One. The Father has expressed Himself fully, and that expression, that Word, has its own eternal existence within the Godhead as a second Person. Christians do not pretend to understand this, but they do believe it, for nothing less can adequately account for the data of Scripture and their experience of the God revealed therein. We have tried to provide at least a glimpse at some of the reasons why in this exposition of the Creed. And there is a third Person as well: We believe in the Holy Spirit, the Lord and giver of life, who proceeds from the Father and the Son and is to be worshipped together with them.

Christians do not believe in the Trinity simply in order to make life—or even doctrine—difficult for themselves or for others. They are simple folk, but they insist on believing the truth, even if it is bigger than what their finite minds can easily grasp. And they are confronted by a God who exists as eternal Father but who became incarnate as a Man without ceasing to be the eternal Father—a Man who prayed to that Father as if He were a distinct Person while claiming at the same time to be One with Him. And then this Man returns to the Father, to sit at His right hand, and sends from there a Comforter who also has all the attributes of deity. All this He does without the least hint of a compromise to the radical monotheism of His Jewish heritage.

Heretics insist on reducing this stubborn and recalcitrant Reality to something their minds can grasp, thereby sacrificing elements essential to biblical religion. Christians simply accept it humbly as the way God is. It is not contradictory, as if they were saying that there was one god and three gods at the same time. But it is mysterious: one God in three Persons. They know that if human beings could understand Him perfectly, they would be understanding something less than God. Not only does Scripture teach them this, but they know this complexly simple God in their own experience every time they pray. To put it into words at all oversimplifies it, but there it is: the Father above them, the Son beside them, and the Spirit within them, groaning with prayers too deep for words. So they also believe in God the Holy Spirit.

God the Father is also Spirit, and God the Son is also Holy. But the Third Person is called the Holy Spirit perhaps because these titles are true of Him while the Analogies by which we know the other two do not quite work for Him. He is the Person who comes least into focus, who stays more mysterious, who hovers, as it were, in the theological background of the group portrait Scripture presents. And this is the way He wants it. For as the Son's meat and drink is to do the will of the Father (Jn. 4:34), so the Spirit's is to glorify the Son (Jn. 16:14).

The Holy Spirit was active in the creation as he brooded over the surface of the waters to bring order and life to the as yet barren world. He is associated with the inspiration of prophets and of Scripture, with conviction, calling, regeneration, sanctification, providing gifts for ministry to the Church. But His central purpose is to bring glory to the Son, by representing the Son in the lives of believers as His personal Agent between the His Ascension and His Return. This perspective indeed brings unity to the seemingly varied range of the Spirit's activities. Revealing Christ, predicting Christ, empowering Christ during His earthly ministry, calling to Christ, joining to Christ, building up in Christ until we attain to complete unity with Christ: truly, Christians confess their belief in the Holy Spirit because they are Christocentric people. For the Spirit is, as it were, the Christocentric member of the Trinity. Blessed be He.

PRAYER: Father, with Thy Spirit's voice and by His power I call Thee Abba. His light reveals and banishes my darkness. His love casts out my fear. His presence makes me desire to see Jesus, who said I could ask for more of Him and would not be disappointed; and so I ask. Amen.

Dominum
"Lord"

Though the title is more closely associated with the Son, the Spirit is also called *kurios, dominus,* Lord: by Paul in 2 Cor. 3:17, and by the Creed as well. He is the Lord and Giver of life. As God He has His own sovereignty in Himself, but as the personal Representative and Agent of the Son, He operates at the behest of, in the name of, and with the authority of the Lord Jesus Christ. Either way, He is properly called Lord.

The sovereignty of the Spirit is a doctrine we need to be reminded of in this theological landscape we inhabit, replete with movements and styles of piety that treat Him as if He were some sort of cosmic Vending Machine dispensing ecstatic experiences by formula in response to anyone who can summon up enough "coins" of subjective "faith." We need to remember that, like the wind, He blows where He will (Jn. 3:8); that He dispenses His spiritual gifts to each believer according to His agenda, not ours (1 Cor. 12:11). For one of us arbitrarily to elevate one of those gifts into a criterion of superior spirituality contrary to the express instructions of the Apostle the Spirit inspired, or to urge our followers to importune the Spirit that He give to each of them that specific gift (1 Cor. 12, 14), is simply a denial of His sovereignty, and hence not only unbiblical but, to speak plainly, heretical. For since the Spirit is in His central role the Agent of Christ, to deny His sovereignty is also to deny the sovereignty of our Lord.

The sovereignty of the Spirit, coupled with His role in conviction, calling, and regeneration, brings us afresh into contact with the awesome mystery of salvation. For while we are confronted with the claims of Christ and the command to repent and believe (Mk 1:15), many are called but few are chosen (Mt. 20:16, 22:14), and none can come unless the Father Himself draws them through the Spirit (Jn. 6:44). If the natural man does not receive the things of the Spirit of God and is incapable of knowing them (1 Cor. 2:14), then how can anyone be saved? We are left with the humbling realization that, while we may well have chosen Christ, it was only because He had in some sense first chosen us; that, left to ourselves, we could not even have made that choice. For salvation is by grace alone and comes to us by faith, and even that faith is not of ourselves but is the gift of God lest any man should boast (Eph, 2:8–10). So the very faith in Christ that we confess when we recite the Creed, the very faith that saves us, is itself the gift of the sovereign Spirit. Why did it come to us, we must wonder? For we were no less unworthy than others passed over. And there is no answer except His sovereignty and His grace. Blessed be He.

The sovereignty of the Spirit makes us shudder at the precipice from which God and God alone has pulled us back. For we would have blithely walked right over it, secure in our waywardness, if left to ourselves. But it also gives great comfort, for the same God who sent His Son to redeem us and His Spirit to create in us saving faith in that Son has also sent the same Spirit to indwell us and to seal us in that faith (Eph. 1:13–14). It is His faithfulness, not mine, that is the guarantee that I will not only be pulled back but kept back from that awful cliff. It is ultimately, therefore, not only because Jesus is Lord but also because the Spirit is Lord as well that we can say, "I know whom I have believed, and am persuaded that He is able to keep that which I've committed unto Him against that day" (2 Tim. 1:12).

PRAYER: Father, we cannot tell the whence or the whither of His movements, and those who are born of Him have that same mystery about them. Help me to save my life by giving up to Him the desire for safe predictability, losing it to His sovereign rule. Amen.

Et Vivificantem
"And Giver of Life"

The Holy Spirit is the Lord and Giver of Life. He hovered over the barren and lifeless chaos of Creation in the beginning, and it gave birth to order, light, and life (Gen. 1:2). When God takes away the spirits of the animals, they die and return to dust; but when He sends forth His Spirit, they are created, springing forth into new life (Ps. 104:30). And therefore when sinners who are dead in their trespasses and sins put their faith in Christ, it is by the Holy Spirit that they are made spiritually alive again (Eph. 2:1, 5).

Life is indeed one of the greatest of mysteries. We know it by its effects, but have a hard time defining its essence. What exactly is it that is missing from the corpse that was alive a few minutes ago? Nothing physical that one can put one's finger on. We can see that life is active, death inert; that life grows, but death decays; that life reproduces itself after its kind though in infinite variety, while death drags all that variety down to the most basic of common denominators as dust returns to dust. But what is this thing that makes such a difference? One can juggle the chemicals forever, stir the soup into just the right mix, and still be left with a mix of chemicals that will not come to life.

Physical life is a miracle. By cloning it we have only copied a miracle, like the Egyptian wizards who reproduced Moses' signs. And if we ever do succeed in creating it in the test tube, this will not cease to be true. For we still will only have followed in the footsteps of the Spirit who gave it to the world in the first place, and even then not without His aid.

But if physical life is a miracle, not capable of existing without the work of the divine Spirit, then what shall we say about spiritual life? "In the day thou eatest thereof," said God to Adam, "thou shalt surely die." And Adam's descendants since the Fall are described by Scripture as dead—not sick, not even mortally ill, but dead—in their trespasses and sins (Eph. 2:1). The Natural Man does not receive the things of the spirit, and therefore cannot know them (1 Cor. 2:14). The faculty by which he might have responded to God is dead; it is a non-functioning, vestigial organ. So, like a radio-controlled plane whose receiver is dead, he veers off on his own. Whether he oppresses his fellows wickedly, wastes his life in profligacy, or builds great systems of morality and great civilizations, he does it his own way, for his own ends, his own glory. This is the sum of human history; this is who we know ourselves to be apart from Christ.

And then, inexplicably, we find ourselves spun around and heading in a new direction. The Christ who seemed either irrelevant or a crutch for the weak becomes the supremely desirable One in all the world, the light of whose glory reflected in created things alone makes them desirable too. Thus the abstract philosophical deity that we invoked at weddings and funerals as simply a part of our cultural heritage becomes a living Person who permeates every moment of life. The mind once emptily cruising through life or full of clever plans for its own advancement finds itself sitting at the feet of a first-century Carpenter drinking in the words of a wisdom that sounds like ultimate folly to its former companions. The heart that either despaired of pleasing God, was unconcerned about it, or assumed self-righteously that of course it was acceptable to a reasonable and indulgent grandfather in heaven finds itself weeping at the foot of the Cross, in rapt adoration and worship of the God of Grace, of *unmerited* favor.

Every single Christian believer who affirms the Creed with understanding is a miracle of new life more astounding than the new-born babies we lightly and metaphorically call miracles. For the Spirit of Christ is indeed the Lord and Giver of Life. Blessed be He.

PRAYER: Father, that consciousness of Thee, that awareness of Christ, that glad turning Godward is the effect of Thy Spirit's brooding wings over my nascent life. May His quickening power increasingly urge me on towards Thee and Thine. Amen.

Qui … Procedit
"Who … Proceedeth"

The Trinity is not a redundancy. Though all three Persons are One, each is unique in Himself and has a unique role to play in God's relations with His creation. This uniqueness is reflected in—or maybe stems from—the relationships they have with each other. The Father is not called the First Person arbitrarily: He is the Fountain (the "*Fons Trinitatis*") from Whom the others eternally flow. But even that flowing is not a redundancy, but differs in nature and quality according to the natures and roles of the Persons. The Son is *begotten*; hence He is called the Son, and the process by which His identity expresses itself in the Godhead is called *filiation*. The Spirit is not the Son, and hence is not begotten. The best verb the Nicene Fathers could find for the process of His self-expression was *proceeding*, the noun *procession*.

Both filiation and procession are mysterious, eternal processes by which God has always been becoming differentiated in terms of Person while remaining one God. Athanasius uses the analogy of a river whose tributary is distinct in identity but part of the same single flow of water as well. Three *hypostases*, one *ousia*, three Persons, one God, three rivers, one watershed? No analogy of course is adequate for such things, but it gives us an idea.

The difference between filiation and procession is not easy to define, indeed may not be definable. But that does not mean that it is either meaningless or unimportant. The Son, by being begotten, provides us with help in relating to God as Father that comes from within the very Godhead itself. This, surely, we need, both as finite and as fallen. The Spirit, by proceeding, perhaps, gives us help in relating to both Father and Son as God that comes from within the very Godhead itself. And this too we need, both as finite and as fallen. No bridge can be built from the finite to the infinite, for addition can go on forever without getting any closer to infinity. Therefore, if we are to relate to such a One at all, He must stoop to us. For only One that high could stoop so low. And He does it in His own unique, Trinitarian, non-redundant fashion.

If we have tried to grasp the significance of the procession of the Spirit in terms of how it impacts us, this is not because we think that it is properly or essentially defined with reference to us, nor that such a definition either exhausts or is even sufficient to the reality. But how else are we to relate to God, except as He relates to us? To attempt to explain what the Trinitarian existence of God means to Him as God in Himself would be hubris at best and insanity easily. But we do have hints, hints that this inconceivably transcendent reality is coherent with God as we know Him. And they are all summed up in the biblical phrase, "God is love."

"God is love." Not simply that He loves, but that He is love in His essence. This does not predicate of the Deity a kind of cosmic mushiness or sentimentality, but rather a concrete and definite relatedness which has all the particularity of the unique relationships we call friend, lover, brother, father, son. Rather, their particularity, their peculiar tang, derives from the ultimate concreteness of this love of God, this love which is God, which to Him is filiation and procession and to us is revelation, incarnation, sacrifice, and regeneration. And which fills all of creation with His glory. For the Spirit proceeds from the Father and the Son.

PRAYER: Father, for Thee to be one with is to be first separate from us. Grant that the distinction and differentiation by which I know myself to be a self may be given the distinction and differentiation of His new creation so I may become my true self in Him. Amen.

Filioque
"... From the Father *and the Son*"

There may be no more controversial and weighted word in all of theology than this seemingly innocent tetrad of syllables, "*filioque*." It means "and the Son," and its insertion into the Western version of the Creed by the Synod of Toledo in 589 helped to occasion the division of Christendom into East and West. For the Orthodox churches of the East, the Spirit proceeds only from the Father; in the West, He is conceived as proceeding from the Father *and* the Son. Now, it is not a good thing either to divide the Church or to make the doctrine of the Trinity even more abstruse than it already is. And many people today cannot see that insisting on this word accomplishes anything beyond these two highly dubious goals. So we must ask whether it is Scripturally justified and whether it really makes a difference.

The biblical basis for the *filioque* lies in the fact that the Spirit is spoken of as the Spirit of Christ as well as the Father, in Rom. 8:9 and Gal. 4:6, and that He is sent by the Son as well as the Father, in Jn. 15:26. The Spirit is the Spirit of Christ (this is called the "genitive relationship"), but Christ is never spoken of as the Christ of the Spirit; the Spirit is sent by the Son, but the Son is not sent by the Spirit. Yet both come from and are sent by the Father. So the *filioque* can be said simply to summarize in one word the biblical data concerning the inter-relationships of the Persons.

Does it really matter? Well, yes. The structure of the relationships between the Persons is less hierarchically articulated in the East than in the West. We all agree that the Persons are equal in essence, power, dignity, and glory. But the West has a more highly developed sense of their subordination to each other in function or role. The Western Trinity is more Christocentric, the Eastern more egalitarian, as a result. The Holy Spirit has less of a supporting role in the East; He gets equal billing with Christ, as it were. And this has interesting consequences. The West tends to a more rational, the East a more mystical approach to the Christian life. The West has a greater emphasis on forensic justification in its understanding of salvation; the East focuses more on *theosis*, the process of becoming like God. All this flows more or less inevitably from the presence or absence of this one seemingly inconsequential little word.

Now, whether these differences are worth dividing the Church over is a difficult call. Scripture surely teaches both the equality of the Persons in the Trinity and their differentiation; it teaches both the validity and importance of reason and its limitations; it teaches both justification and sanctification. So are we talking about merely a matter of emphasis? Well, even matters of emphasis can be important. We want to have the emphasis that Scripture has, the concept of the relationship between Christ and the Spirit that the Son and the Spirit have. And the Son, who surely knows the Spirit best, has defined that for us: "He shall glorify me" (Jn. 16:14). That is the role the Spirit *wants* to have. John the Baptist was the only man of whom it is said that he was filled with the Spirit from his mother's womb. And he shows it by adopting the Spirit's attitude toward the Son: "He must increase, but I must decrease" (Jn. 3:30). That is the authentic voice of the Holy Spirit speaking.

The supporting role rather than equal billing, in other words, is the role that the Holy Spirit wants. Biblical faith *is* Christocentric, and nobody pursues that Christocentric agenda more zealously than the Spirit Himself. I do not personally feel any need to anathematize my Eastern brethren for omitting the *filioque* from their version of the Creed. But as it helps me to affirm these important truths, I will continue to use the Western formula when I confess my own faith. For that, I believe, is most pleasing to the Spirit. May Christ receive the glory.

PRAYER: Father, the Spirit in me has this effect: I know something of Christ's Life newly incarnated in me because of Bethlehem; crucifixion has a reality in my everyday life because of Golgotha; and hints of my own Easter break through because of the Empty Tomb. "Receive the Spirit," He said afterwards, and breathed on them. And so may I receive. Amen.

Qui cum Patre et Filio
"Who, with the Father and the Son …"

Having adequately stressed the differentiation between the Persons of the Trinity in its discussion of the Spirit, the Creed rounds off this section by returning to their unity. Like the Son, who is begotten by the Father but is one with the Father, who is both with God and is God, the Spirit who proceeds from the Father and the Son is not separate from them but exists together with them as one God. The Spirit, though subordinate to the Father and the Son in function or role, is equal with them in essence, and quite specifically is to receive with them equal adoration and glory, the adoration and glory proper to God.

We are reminded that, while biblical religion is properly Christocentric, we are never to create dichotomies in our understanding of the Trinity that pit one of the Persons against the others or that seem to put them in competition for our adoration or even attention. Some theologies (classical liberalism, deism) tend to reduce God to the Father, being functionally unitarian or modalistic despite their occasional token nods to orthodoxy. Some theologies (older dispensationalism, cessationism) tend almost to ignore the role of the Spirit in our redemption, while others (Pentecostalism, some parts of the Charismatic movement) are so oriented toward it that their most pressing question is not "Do you know the Lord," but "Have you received the Spirit?" Yet he who does not have the Spirit of Christ does not belong to Him (Rom. 8:9). Some theologies (some versions of Pentecostalism and the Wesleyan holiness tradition) speak as if the work of Christ can be divided—as if Christ saves but the Spirit sanctifies, Christ redeems but the Spirit empowers. But nothing could be farther from the biblical perspective, in which the whole work of redemption is performed by Christ and applied by the Spirit to His people on His behalf.

The Spirit is the personal Agent and Representative of Christ, who represents Him in the lives of His people by indwelling them until He returns. In conviction, calling, regeneration, illumination, sanctification, He carries on the work of Christ, not some other superadded or extra work of His own. In the prologue to his sequel, Luke aptly refers to his former book, the Gospel, as the story of all that Jesus began to do and teach, thus implying that Acts, the book of the Holy Spirit par excellence, is the story of what Jesus *continued* to do. And continues to do today, through the Spirit because He was sent by Jesus and the Father.

The whole Trinity is then to be worshipped together because God is one. Their roles are distinct, but they act in concert. The Father initiates, the Son accomplishes, the Spirit applies. We pray to the Father in the name of the Son with the aid of the Spirit. The Father is above us, the Son beside us, the Spirit within us. Each Person is present at every point. And while the Spirit prefers to direct our attention toward the Son and the Son points us to the Father, we would know none of them nor be able to love and serve God at all were it not for the work of all three. So therefore the enabling Spirit is to be acknowledged as present and active and relevant in our homage to the Son and the Father. Indeed, He is essential to it, and should therefore be neither pressed out of His preferred supporting role into the foreground or center stage, nor forgotten. He is equally God, together with the Father and the Son.

PRAYER: Father, the fears within and the fightings without, the experience of things in contentious competition, distort my conception of both the distinctions and the unity which is the Godhead. Be Thou my vision so that what is different and what is the same may bring their healing beauty and strength into my corruption and weakness. Amen.

Simul Adoratur
"Is to be Adored"

The Spirit, together with the Father and the Son, is to be worshipped, literally adored. But modern connotations of the word *adore,* while not irrelevant, are perhaps too mushy and sentimental to be fully accurate. *Adorare* comes from two Latin words meaning literally "speak to." In context, it means to speak to God, hence pray, supplicate, worship. It translates one of the Greek words for worship, *proskuneo,* which means "kiss toward," referring to the subject who makes obeisance to an oriental potentate, as if kissing his feet or the ground on which he walks. Perhaps in that verbal picture we can see both the point and the inadequacy of connecting this Latin word for worship with its modern English descendant.

The English word *worship* itself comes from the Anglo-Saxon *weorthscipe,* literally worth-ship. It denotes the act of ascribing worth: "Thou art worthy O Lord to receive majesty and glory and honor and dominion and power." Whatever word we use, worship is the act or process by which the creature and the sinner orients itself rightly and properly toward its Creator and Redeemer. In prayer, praise, the proclamation of Scripture, the offering up of our gifts and of our selves, in Baptism and in the fellowship of the Lord's Table, we encounter, we contemplate, and we declare God's worth and our unworthiness, His greatness and our weakness, His holiness and our sinfulness, His mercy and our repentance, His grace and our acceptance of that grace and hence our joy. Worship is the cultivation and expression, guided by Scripture and the wisdom of Christian tradition, of the attitudes appropriate to the One who is the object of our adoration, of the response His inherent worthiness deserves from us. And by expressing those attitudes, worship reinforces them: the Godward focus, even as we necessarily abase ourselves before His greatness, orients us toward His grace as well, and thus deepens our lives, increases our capacity for that grace, and ennobles us. We never stand taller in the order of creation than when we are on our faces at His feet.

We are then to worship and adore the whole Trinity, the Spirit together with the Father and the Son. This affirmation tells us something about God and something about worship. We confess that the Spirit is, like the Son, fully God, in that He is to be worshipped together with the Father and the Son. He is neither a vague force nor merely the personification of God's power, but a living Person who is one with the Father and the Son.

And we confess by implication that true worship is what the Son said it is: worship in spirit and in truth. Worship that is not conscious of the whole range of Christian doctrine in the fullness of its Trinitarian glory is worship that is less than fully Christian. None of us understands God fully or ever worships Him worthily. By His grace he accepts and deigns even to be pleased by our poor and inadequate worship, but only by His grace. Still, for that very reason, we must give Him our best. And therefore, if the Church is to worship the Spirit together with the Father and the Son, it is incumbent upon it to teach the theology behind its Creed with consistency, clarity, and power. The modern world's sensibilities may think doctrine dry and intellectual, hence inimical to its debased concept of worship, or irrelevant to it at best. But if we are to offer up to Him our whole person, we must offer up also our minds. And if we confess the faith with understanding, we realize that in reality doctrine, yea even the difficult doctrine of the Trinity, is the very foundation on which true adoration of God must inevitably rest.

PRAYER: Father, He said to the Woman at the Well, "Ye worship ye know not what." Grant that my worship may be grounded in a true knowing of Thee in the community of Thyself and in the knowledge that all such knowing is Thy gift to me through Jesus by the Spirit. Amen.

Et Conglorificatur
"And Glorified Together"

Together with the Father and the Son, the Spirit is to be glorified. This word amplifies the point that the Trinity is to be adored or worshipped. What does it add?

We have already defined the glory of God as the manifestation in the created world of the majestic reality of His perfect character in all of its awesome splendor. That is glory as it appears to human beings. In itself, it is central to all God's attributes, perhaps best described as the sum of them. So in one sense it is rather strange to speak of worship as giving glory to God. One might just as well give it out as one's opinion that there ought to be three sides to a triangle or 360 degrees to a circle. God has glory as an innate and inalienable possession. Nothing we could possibly do could add the least scintilla to its brightness or subtract the most minute measure of magnitude from its radiance. Such was the glory He had before the world was; so He still dwells in unimaginable splendor and unapproachable light.

Yet we do not ascribe all glory and honor and power to each member of the Trinity because they need to be reminded of it, or to fill up any lack in the glory that is theirs. It is we who need to acknowledge this greatest and most sublime of realities, to have our heads lifted up out of the mundane clutter that surrounds and fills them and have them reoriented to this piercing light before which even the Angels are abashed. It is we who need to be reinvigorated by the paradoxical knowledge that, while our place before Him is in our faces on the dust, this very abasement ennobles us more than any scrambling for our own honor ever could.

It is impossible ever to fully appreciate the privilege that is ours when this exalted Being calls us servant, son, daughter, friend. But it is impossible even to approach any understanding of it at all, to catch the faintest glimmer of what we owe to His grace, until we begin to appreciate the blinding glory He cloaks in human flesh in becoming incarnate so we can relate to Him, the dizzying height from which He stoops in condescension to us. And therefore we fulfill our own natures in worship precisely because worship involves the reverent contemplation of His great glory, the glad and awed affirmation of His incomprehensible worthiness, a hushed awe at the fact that He is large enough to be mindful of we who are so small, the jubilant celebration of all the He is in himself and the wonder of all that He is to us.

As Jesus faced the Cross, He prayed, "Father, the hour is come. Glorify the Son, that the Son may glorify thee" (Jn. 17:1). In nothing is His glory more profoundly revealed than in His stooping to save us. Nowhere do we get a fuller revelation of who and what He is. Nothing, in other words, more exalts Him than that stooping. And so nothing more exalts us than the act of bowing in awe and submission before the One who stooped to us. It was the Father who sent, the Son who came, and the Spirit who empowered Him to bear the unbearable burden of our sin. Without all three, the Glory would have remained hidden and unexpressed. Without all three, in other words, we would have remained in darkness. And so it is good and right and necessary that the Spirit be glorified together with the Father and the Son.

PRAYER: Father, Thou hast made me with the capacity to reflect Thee and so extend Thy glory as a mirror extends light. But, without Thy salvation, I not only see through a glass darkly, I am a glass darkened. Let this salvation so cleanse that my life may glorify Thee by reflecting Thy glory in all my thinking, saying, and doing. Amen.

Qui Locutus Est
"Who Spake ..."

The Creed concludes its section on the Spirit by reminding us that He is articulate: He spoke through the prophets. The first thing God does in Scripture is to create, and the second is to speak; or we might more accurately give honor of place to both together, since He spoke the world into existence. "And He said, 'Let there be light,' and there was light." With language He summons things into existence, differentiates and organizes them ("And He separated the light from the darkness"), and gives them meaning and value ("And God saw that it was good"). Then He makes Man in His own image (Gen. 1). And the first thing we do is start talking too.

The creation story, in other words, presents God as implicitly omnipotent (for He made every other power), omnipresent (for He made space), omniscient (for He designed everything else that exists), and eternal (for He made time as we know it). But above all, and explicitly, it presents Him as Personal and Relational. For language is the means of all these other accomplishments, and it is by language that He manifests His kinship with us. He speaks of all the other creatures in that account in the third person: "Let there be ... let them ..." But He addresses Adam as *thou*. And Adam responds.

This personal articulateness is central to the whole Trinity. The Second Person is called the *Logos*, the Word (Jn. 1:1). Among the most memorable parts of His earthly ministry are the marvelous words He left behind, for He spoke as no other man has ever spoken (Jn. 7:46). After two thousand years He is still the greatest composer of parables in the whole history of literature. Nobody else even comes close. And when He returned to the Father, He left His own Spokesman behind in One who had already announced His coming as Herald of old: The Holy Spirit, who spoke though the prophets and would now speak through the apostles as well.

That God's first act was speech because His nature is speech (the *logos*) may be one of the most profound revelations about Him that Scripture gives us. It is the essence of personality, the impulse to self revelation. He imparts this character in a rudimentary way to everything that He makes, and in its greatest fullness to human beings. No one has seen this more clearly than Gerard Manley Hopkins:

> As kingfishers catch fire, dragonflies draw flame;
> As tumbled over rim in roundy wells
> Stones ring; like each tucked string tells, each hung bell's
> Bow swung finds tongue to fling out broad its name;
> Each mortal thing does one thing and the same:
> Deals out that being indoors each one dwells;
> Selves—goes itself; *myself* it speaks and spells,
> Crying *What I do is me: for that I came.*
>
> I say more: the just man justices;
> Keeps grace: that keeps all his goings graces;
> Acts in God's eye what in God's eye he is—
> Christ—for Christ plays in then thousand places,
> Lovely in limbs and lovely in eyes not his
> To the Father though the features of men's faces.

All this self revelation, dumb in the other physical creatures, articulate in Man, exists because God is a God who speaks.[1]

PRAYER: Father, let my life be no uncertain sound, no gong, no tinkling cymbal, but let my speech echo Thy character as one becoming Thine. May His creative Voice give me the words to say when brought before fellow-man magistrate, His own grace-seasoned answers to my hope in Christ. Amen.

Per Prophetas
"Through the Prophets"

While the prophets and apostles spoke in their own voices, it was also the Holy Spirit who spoke through them. Paul says that all Scripture is inspired by God (2 Tim. 3:16). Literally, he says that the very words on the page, the "writings" (*ta graphe*) were breathed out (*theopneustos*) by God. As a result, though they are still the words of Moses, David, Isaiah, Paul, Luke, etc., chosen by them (except for isolated passages dictated like the Decalogue) and expressing their individual personalities, they are also the words of God, and therefore authoritative, inerrant, infallible, and profitable for doctrine, reproof, correction, and training in righteousness. How can this be?

Well, suppose I ask my secretary to write a memo. I could dictate the very words myself, as God apparently did with the Ten Commandments and certain passages in the prophets. Or I could let her compose it, with complete freedom to choose every word as she sees fit according to her own gifts and personality. She might even do research, as Luke did (1:1–4), to figure out what she wants to say. I might then revise what she wrote or decide that it expressed my intentions without need of revision. In any case, once I had signed the document, the words would count as mine, however they were produced. They would have my authority and they would speak for me. A discerning reader might be able to distinguish the memos I dictated from the ones that were written by Melissa, and those from the ones produced by her predecessors, Kristi and Amanda. But if I had signed them, they would all equally be my words. We can say that God "signed" the books of Scripture, as it were, by providentially having them included in the canon.

Thus, the God who spoke the world into existence, who spoke it also into form and value, continues to speak to His people today, because the

Holy Spirit of old spoke through the prophets. And faithful Christians continue to hear His voice as well as theirs in their writings. They therefore believe these words and obey them. They do not pretend that there are no problems in the texts as we have them. They do not pretend that they can reconcile all the apparent discrepancies or demonstrate independently the truth of every individual biblical assertion. They are well aware of the stupidities perpetrated by well-meaning believers who have ignored context, genre, and common sense, and then asserted their ill-advised interpretations as if *they* were absolute truth. They are painfully aware of their own capacity for such folly. But they attribute all such problems to their own ignorance or faulty understanding rather than to the text of Scripture itself. Advances in knowledge have confirmed the wisdom of this attribution over and over. "Errors" in the Text are shown to be gaps in our knowledge or assumptions produced by secular world views or theories advanced by scholars on the basis more of speculation than fact. The apparent discrepancies that remain affect no doctrine, and are properly referred to as "problems" rather than "errors." For the faithful approach is both reasonable and right if indeed the Holy Spirit spoke through the prophets.

God still speaks in the Text. He teaches, promises, warns, predicts, describes, evaluates, commands, communes. And the Church listens, learns, obeys, proclaims, communes, and worships. And it distills the teaching of Scripture into the Creed; and it confesses. All this it does because God spoke light into the primal darkness, and the Son is *logos,* and the Spirit spoke through the prophets.

Hear them!

For more on the doctrine of inspiration and the work of the Holy Spirit in general, see the author's book *The Person and Work of the Holy Spirit* (Nashville: Broadman, 1994; Rpt. Wipf & Stock).

PRAYER: Father, to stand alone on the Word of God is to know it to be the Book for me, to know that these words are His words to me, the words of life. Let me occupy myself with them always, thereby fastening them to the agent of thinking, my forehead, and the agents of doing, my hands. Amen.

IV
THE CHURCH

Et in Unum ... Ecclesiam
"And in One ... Church"

Having confessed our faith in God as the Father, the Son, and the Holy Spirit, we turn at last to consider the Community of Faith doing the confessing. It is called the Church, the *ekklesia,* a Greek word meaning the "called out" or gathered ones, the assembly. From the Greek word and its Latin counterpart we get the English *ecclesiastical* (having to do with the Church) and *ecclesiology* (the doctrine of the Church). The English *church* actually comes from a different Greek word, *kuriakon,* which means "belonging to the Lord." So the Church is that group of people, at a given time and place or throughout history, who have been called by the Lord and thus belong to Him. It is an organization (or a collection of organizations) but first an organism, an institution but first a family, a guardian of tradition because first it is a confessing and worshipping Community. And according to our confession it is one, holy, catholic (or universal), and apostolic.

But before we apply those adjectives to the Church, we had better be clear about what it is in itself. It was founded by the Lord Himself on Peter's confession that Jesus is the Christ, the Son of the Living God (Mt. 16:16–18). Why do we say on Peter's confession, not Peter himself as our Roman Catholic brothers allege? For three reasons. First, there are two different Greek words used in Mt. 16:16, distinguishing Peter (a stone) from the rock (i.e., boulder) on which the Church is founded. Second, Paul tells us in Eph. 2:20 that the Church is built on the foundation of the prophets and apostles (plural), with Christ Himself as the Cornerstone. And finally, Peter does not seem to have viewed himself as uniquely foundational to the Church, agreeing with Paul that Christ is the Cornerstone (1 Pet. 2:6) and seeing himself only as a "fellow elder" (5:1). Surely Peter as its original recipient would be the best witness to the meaning of the Lord's cryptic utterance of Mt. 16.

Peter therefore has "primacy" only in the sense that he was the first to make the Confession which anchors and defines the Community. What is central to it is not his leadership or that of his successors but the confession that Jesus is the Christ. For by that Confession its true members live, and for it they would lay down their lives. So they are called together by the Spirit of Christ to nurture and encourage one another in it, to proclaim it, and to work out its implications in the whole of their lives until the Christ they confess returns.

The New Testament uses a number of metaphors to give us the idea of what this Community is all about. It is the Household or Family of God, the Pillar and Support of the Truth (I Tim. 3:15, Eph. 2:19). It is an eternal Temple to the glory of Christ, in which the Saints are set as living stones (Eph. 2:21, I Pet. 2:5). It is a kingdom of priests (1 Pet. 2:5, 9), representing God to the world. Above all, it is the Body of Christ (1 Cor. 12:27, Eph. 4:15–16, etc.). By this we understand that the Church is the primary means by which Christ ministers in the world, that He is the Head of it and intimately or organically related to it as such, and that as members of it we should care for one another as even the members of our own bodies do, giving the greater honor to the weak and lowly.

How do these exalted descriptions relate to the motley crew of believers who inhabit the steeple-crowned buildings that dot our street-corners? How should we relate to those buildings, those people, and these descriptions? We confess that such a Church exists and that it is one, holy, catholic, and apostolic. Perhaps in those affirmations lie some answers.

PRAYER: Father, what makes us Church is that He is building us. What makes us one is His breaking down of that which divided us. What makes us grow is His provision in what every joint supplies. May my life be witness to His building, His tearing down of barriers, and His supply for all His He brings my way. Amen.

Unum
"One"

Perhaps no affirmation of the Creed more seriously taxes our ability to walk by faith and not by sight than the claim that the Church is "one." Sight seems to contradict us at every turn. Literally thousands of splintered organizations, each jealously guarding its own versions and perversions of the Tradition, glare suspiciously at their neighbors from behind barricaded doors. East vs. West, Protestant vs. Catholic, Lutheran vs. Reformed vs. Arminian, Episcopalian vs. Presbyterian vs. Congregationalist, Traditional vs. Pentecostal—the lists go on. I can think of eleven different breeds of Baptist off the top of my head. The world has some excuse if it looks at us with a bit of skeptical confusion on this point.

One strategy adopted by a number of these organizations in an effort to deal with this problem is to claim—sometimes explicitly, sometimes only implicitly—that "*we* are the one true Church, and all the others are illegitimate—phonies, counterfeits, apostates." Such a claim may be based on being the oldest, with the most continuity to the past, or on being the newest and most purified and restored, or just being the most biblical (according to their own understanding of the Bible, of course). They all claim that there is really only one true Church, and they are it. But how are we to know which if any of these claims are valid? Each claimant will tell you that theirs is, by their criteria. Naturally.

Part of the difficulty is that it is easy to beg the question what the Bible means by oneness. The Apostle Paul speaks of preserving the unity of the Spirit in the bond of peace because there is one body. This he parallels with one hope of our calling, one Lord, one faith, one baptism, one God and Father of all (Eph. 4:3–6). What are these? One Lord, Jesus Christ; one faith, the faith once delivered to the saints, summarized in the ecumenical creeds; one baptism, a baptism of repentance for the remission of sins. Surely the burden of proof would be on anyone who would identify them otherwise.

Note: no mention is made of one organizational structure. No doubt it would be nice in some ways if we still had that luxury, but history has obliterated it, and no amount of wishing, however pious, will bring it back. In fact, as things stand, it might have its disadvantages. As Milton reminds us in "Areopagetica," until there is agreement, it is better that many be tolerated than all compelled.[1] But there is still, thank God, one Lord, one faith, one baptism.

Wherever people confess that Jesus Christ is Lord, that He died for our sins, and that God has raised Him from the dead; wherever they are baptized in the name of the Trinity as an expression of repentance and the hope of forgiveness; wherever they gather around His Table; wherever, in other words, the Gospel is rightly preached and the Sacraments rightly administered, there is the true Body of Christ. It does not matter what name is above the door, what idiosyncrasies have accrued, or what imperfections in manifestation have appeared. All who confess the faith that this Creed delineates are our Christian brothers and sisters, and we share a unity with them that transcends our denominational differences. And this is just as true as the fact that, in our sinfulness, we often broadcast our denominational chauvinism much more loudly.

This transcendent unity, all true Believers have experienced. To find more convincing ways of manifesting that unity before the world is the challenge which faces all those who confess that they believe in One Church.

PRAYER: Father, move us by Thy Spirit and in the love of Jesus toward the answer to His petition that all His may be one as You are One. Help me to fix my eyes on Him and, in so drawing nigh to Thee, draw nigh to all of Thine. Amen.

Sanctam
"Holy"

The first truth about the Church we must accept by faith is its unity; the second is its holiness. And faith as opposed to sight—at least on the surface—may be just as requisite here. How in the world can these groups of often petty, bickering, backbiting players of church politics, these hotbeds of willful ignorance, these congregations of lax and complacent players at ethical brinksmanship despite their insufferable air of smug moral superiority, be accurately described without mortal injury to the English language as *holy*?

Well, the problem did not begin with us. The Apostle Paul had to contend with the church of Corinth: sowers of division, toleraters of incest, addicted to carnality, practicers of disorder of every kind in their public worship, and proud of it. Yet he calls them "the church of God which is at Corinth ... *sanctified* [i.e., *made holy*] in Jesus Christ, called to be *saints* [i.e., *holy ones*]." What kind of gobbledygook or doublespeak is this?

It was just the plain and simple truth.

The true Church is a body of sinners saved by grace. They are not perfect, just forgiven. In God's eyes, they are clothed, not with the filthy rags of their own righteousness, but with the white robes of Christ's. But in this life, two factors keep us from being able to see that vision with clarity.

The first is the fact that the Visible Church is not quite the same as the true or Invisible Church. While the Church is for Believers, and a regenerate membership ought always to be its goal, this is not a goal that is perfectly attainable. There are always going to be tares among the wheat. Many who loudly profess the name of Christ know not what spirit they are of, and are in danger of hearing on the Last Day those awful words, "Depart from me ... I never knew you."

The second is the fact that even the regenerate are not yet perfect. Though they are justified by faith, their sanctification is an ongoing process that will not be complete until they see Christ face to face. They are all in various stages of that journey. The White Robes are theirs already, and will one day be a perfect fit. But for now, the filthy rags are continually showing through beneath, sometimes in the most appalling ways.

Nevertheless, it is a true affirmation when we confess that the Church is holy. For *holy* means, most basically, "set apart." Like the implements in the Temple, Believers have already been set apart from the world, from common use, consecrated to the service of God. Hence the New Testament calls all of them saints or holy ones, not because they are all already very saintly but because, having been thus set apart, sainthood is their destiny. God has already accepted them as holy in Jesus Christ and committed Himself to bring them to actual holiness. And what God has decreed will happen is as good as done. Many of them already show amazing progress in Christlikeness, and we should not lose this fact in the fog generated by the sinfulness remaining in the others. So while the full manifestation of the Church's holiness, the full experience of it, awaits us in the future, we can already refer to it as a present reality. Hence we confess that the true Church is holy.

Because holiness is our identity and our destiny, it is therefore incumbent upon us to remember when we make this confession that it is our duty to walk in a manner worthy of our calling (Eph. 4:1). Thus we would avoid being a stumbling block to the world, and thus we would bring glory to our Lord who bought us. And thus we would live as the true Church indeed.

PRAYER: Father, You made the light, You judged it good, You divided it from darkness, and You called it Day. Even so, You are making Your church, You have judged it good, You are dividing it from that which is less than good, and You have named it Holy. May these realities become increasingly our experience. Amen.

Catholicam
"Universal"

The true Church, we confess, is marked by unity and holiness. It also has the quality of *catholicity*, or universality. It is unfortunate that one denomination, the Church of Rome, has preempted this ancient word as part of its name, giving the impression that it alone truly has this quality. But this is a confession relevant to Protestants as well. So what do we mean when we say that the Church is universal?

For the Church of Rome, catholicity is a part of her apologetic: she can claim to have existed at all times and to be represented in all places in ways that are not so plausible for the various Protestant denominations. But the existence of Orthodoxy, which can equally trace its institutional existence back to apostolic times, belies that claim. And Protestants question whether these attributes of the Church can legitimately be applied to any single institutional organization as such, rather than to the Body of Christ, that spiritual organism which transcends the various denominational structures. Surely it was not the Church of Rome, or Antioch, or Jerusalem individually and separately that possessed catholicity even in New Testament times, not the individual local communities considered in isolation but rather as belonging to the larger whole of which they were all a part.

Yet the true Church, however we identify her, is catholic of necessity, because the God she serves is the Lord of all the earth. Her commission is that, as she spreads through all the earth, she should make disciples of all nations (Mat. 28:19). Her destiny is to include people from every tongue, tribe, and nation (Rev. 5:9). She is a universal Church because her Lord is a universal Lord and her Gospel a universal Gospel. Paul in his most careful extended argument includes all human beings under sin (Rom. 3:9). So all men and women everywhere and at all times are in desperate need of her message. And that message is the power of God unto salvation for all men and women everywhere and at all times, for the Jew first, and also for the Greek (Rom. 1:16). When we confess that she is catholic, then, we remind ourselves that inherent in her very nature and being is the drive, the irresistible impulse, to actualize her universality by spreading herself across the globe, incarnating herself in every society, first in Jerusalem, then in Judaea, then in Samaria, and finally to the uttermost parts of the earth (Acts 1:8). The universal relevance of the Church's message is what impels her toward a universal presence, spread out in space and time like a mighty army with banners flying.

Nothing is more politically incorrect than the Church's claim to universality. Who are we to impose our beliefs on others, to invade and corrupt their cultures? So deeply ingrained is this feeling in our society that it has become Starfleet's "Prime Directive" in our most popular vision of the future. And it is a feeling that seems more catholic and more charitable on the surface. But if human beings are fallen and in need of redemption, and if God has committed the message of that redemption to His Church, then nothing could be less charitable and hence less catholic than the Prime Directive. Who are we to take our way of seeing things to the whole world? People who have been transformed by the Gospel of Jesus Christ, saved from futility and meaninglessness and judgment; beggars who know where to find bread. Seen in this light, we *must* be catholic, or cease to be Christians at all.

PRAYER: Father, let me hear Thee tell the father of the faithful that his children would be as the stars for number, and then let me see that promise fulfilled in my brother's eyes and my sister's smile. Let the expanse of Thy redeemed humanity relieve me of what is mean and miserly in my conception of Thy Kingdom and send me forth as its ambassador. Amen.

Et Apostolicam
"And Apostolic"

The Church of Jesus Christ is one, holy, universal, and *apostolic*. But while all branches of Christendom would make this claim, they do not all understand it in the same way. Some lay great stress on what they call "apostolic succession," the unbroken line of the ordination of bishops by the laying on of hands that stretches all the way back to the Apostles who appointed the first bishops. Others lay greater stress on a different kind of continuity, not of hands but of apostolic doctrine. Christians may disagree as to how far the unbroken line of hands is essential to ensuring the Church's faithfulness to that doctrine; but there can be no controversy that such faithfulness is essential to her identity as the true Church. She is built on the foundation of the prophets and the apostles, Christ Jesus being the Cornerstone (Eph. 2:20). And the Apostle Paul exhorts Timothy, a man on whom his own hands had been laid, "the things that thou hast heard of me among many witnesses, the same commit thou to faithful men, who shall be able to teach others also" (2 Tim. 2:2).

The laying on of hands transmits responsibility for leadership from one generation to the next; teaching transmits the doctrine, both to the leaders and to the whole Church. And it must be the doctrine the Apostles laid down and codified authoritatively in Scripture.

Who were these people who are so important to the Church despite their having crumbled into dust two millennia ago? *Apostolos* is the noun form of *apostello*, which means "I send." So an apostle in general is a messenger or commissioner—"missionary" is not a bad translation—but there were also special Apostles, with a capital A, as it were. These had to be eyewitnesses of the Resurrection who had been appointed by the Lord to be His special representatives during the first generation of Christian witness (Acts 1:22). The eleven surviving Disciples, with the addition of Matthias to replace the traitor Judas, were the original group. Paul, qualified by having seen a post-Resurrection appearance of the Lord on the Damascus Road, became a special apostle for the Gentiles (cf. the openings of his epistles, especially Galatians, and Acts 22:14, 21).

These men devoted themselves to the ministry of the word and prayer (Acts 6:4). They founded churches and appointed elders over them. And they, or men working under their auspices (as in the case of Mark and Luke), wrote the New Testament. During the first generation, their living voice was the touchstone of faithful witness to Christ as Lord. Now, their writings preserved in the New Testament perform that function. So for us to say that a Church is apostolic is to say that its teachings, worship, life, and witness are based on the New Testament. To be apostolic is to be governed by the New Testament, held to it as a standard, and animated by its spirit.

When we confess the Church's apostolicity in the Creed, therefore, we remind ourselves of the importance of the New Testament to the Church's life and identity and recommit ourselves to believing its teachings and living by its commandments, both as individuals and as a body. By the New Testament, the Apostles, being dead, yet speak. By it they continue to rule and guide the Church on behalf of her Lord. When we are faithful to it, we are faithful to them and to Him.

PRAYER: Father, I thank Thee that their words can be counted on, those who saw His tears and sweat, His blood, His face and garments brighter than the noonday sun. Their words I take as milk and meat, as water for washing, and as an edge sharp enough for dividing soul and spirit. Amen.

... *Ecclesiam*
"... Church"

We believe then in one holy, catholic, and apostolic Church. And we promised that examining her unity, holiness, catholicity, and apostolicity might help us learn how to relate to the various forms in which she exists. For while the true or "invisible" Church has all these qualities, none of the forms in which she is encountered as the "visible" Church here and now manifest them perfectly. When you find the perfect church, one wag has said, don't join it; for as a result of that very act it will cease being perfect from that day forth! Yet, if we confess a belief in the Church as part of our Christian credo, we had better be part of that Church. And if none is perfect, how do we choose between the various options, not all of which are equally deserving of our support? And how do we discern those which are not worthy of it at all?

The Creed gives us a set of criteria which have proved their usefulness over time. If we confess that there is one Church, then it would seem to follow that there are two extremes we should avoid. A group which fractures the unity of Christ's Body by loudly proclaiming itself alone as the only valid form of it is suspect, as is one that is unconcerned about the fragmented face that the Church presents to the world. We are looking for a group then that, while holding honestly to its own distinctives, recognizes as true brethren in Christ all those in other groups who do not, but who nonetheless confess the true Faith as summarized by the Creed. And it would care more about its kinship with them than its differences from them, and express that caring in fellowship and practical cooperation with them.

If we confess that the Church is holy, then we are looking for a group that takes seriously the importance of practical godliness, growth in grace, Christlike character. It is not perfect, but it is sensible of the fact that being forgiven sets it on a quest for a life worthy of the Lord who bought it. And because it knows that this holiness comes only by grace and a life of dependence on its Lord, it practices its piety in a way that avoids becoming legalistic or judgmental. That is a balance which is not achievable in the flesh, but which, if we confess the Church's holiness with understanding, is simply not optional for any church that claims to be part of the Church.

If we confess that the Church is catholic, then we are looking for a group that has a worldwide vision and a missionary heart. She is not satisfied to be provincial either in scope or in outlook. She has the courage not to flinch at the absolute and universal claims of the Gospel. Her message is for all people at all times and in all places, not by being generic and bland, but by cutting to the heart of the universal human need for meaning and salvation. And she knows that she can maintain such universal relevance only by being faithful to the Gospel that does not change.

If we confess that the Church is apostolic, then we are looking for a group that believes the Bible unashamedly and without compromise. She is a New-Testament Church, not just as a slogan but in the difficult struggle of faithfulness in understanding and applying to her contemporary situation the message of the Apostles. She thinks that Paul, Matthew, Peter, James, and John know more about the Gospel, its meaning, and how practically to live it out, than she does. So her ministry is centered on the faithful exposition of the whole counsel of God, which she receives as such.

Is what I have described Roman Catholic, Orthodox, Baptist, Methodist, or Presbyterian? One who expects that kind of answer still does not understand. One who confesses the Church with understanding will find a congregation, whatever the name over the door, that manifests these characteristics, and be faithful to it despite its imperfections. And thus we will confess, not only the Church, but also its Lord.

PRAYER: Father, I praise Thee for true indicators of faithfulness in human flesh. Let there be no ambiguity about the balances in which I weigh the worth of things, and therefore no confusion in my allegiance to those who receive my loyalty. Amen.

Confiteor
"I Confess"

We have been talking about confessing from the beginning of this study; now finally the word itself appears. So it would be well to pause on it and discover what it means.

The operative verb at the beginning of the Creed is not confess but *credo,* "I believe." It refers in this context, as we saw, to the act by which one inwardly commits oneself to something as true. But once we profess this inward belief outwardly and publicly—which is what we do even when we say "I *believe* in one God the Father almighty"—then we have moved already from belief to confession, from *credo* to *confiteor. Confiteor* means "I confess" or "acknowledge." When one confesses one's sins to the Lord, a priest, a friend, a congregation, or a court, one acknowledges them, owns up to them, accepts responsibility for them. In confessing our beliefs we do the same thing. We do not just express opinions we happen to hold. We publicly identify ourselves with our deepest beliefs and with the company with whom we share them. We declare our commitment to those people and those beliefs, take our stand behind and under the beliefs and with the people. We profess our conviction of their relevance and importance for others, of our willingness to live by them and die for them. And we rejoice in their truth, celebrate it, and praise God for it. Any less and we perjure ourselves, and had better stay silent rather than babble meaningless noises.

Such confessing is good for the soul, and hence an appropriately essential part of worship. But it is more than that: it is also essential to salvation. "If you confess with your mouth Jesus as Lord," Paul said, "and believe in your heart that God raised him from the dead, you shall be saved. For with the heart man believes unto righteousness, and with the mouth confession is made unto salvation" (Rom. 10:9–10). Not that there is anything magical about the words of the Nicene Creed: it is one ancient, tested, tried, and approved way of making that confession. So is the shorter and earlier creed called the Apostles'. Paul's readers were no doubt making that confession in their own words before either had been composed, and they should continue to do so. What is essential is that condition of mind, heart, and soul of which the act of confessing Christ is the natural expression.

We are saved, more specifically justified, by faith (Rom. 3:28). So why does Paul seven chapters later say that we must not only believe but confess? Because a belief that is content to remain inward only is mere opinion. But saving faith is more: a commitment to Christ, a personal relationship of trust in Him. We are saved, not by holding certain opinions that we might tick off on a survey, but by the relationship of trust that we enter into with Christ when we accept Him as Lord. And this relationship can no more be hidden from the world than a college romance can be hidden from one's fellow students. In fact, when we are truly in love, we *want* to declare it openly before the world, as countless initials carved into countless trees attest. We want to sing the praise of our beloved, to be seen with him or her. True faith, like murder, will out.

Thus, when we rightly confess our faith, the beliefs that are not just our opinions but the content of the saving faith we put in Christ, we are also in a sense confessing our love. We are declaring our marriage vows. Having believed in our hearts that God has raised Him from the dead, we confess Jesus as Lord. And thus we are saved indeed.

PRAYER: Father, overcome by the power of Thy Spirit the fear and unbelief which inhibit my public confession of Thy claim on me. Let all who come in contact with me know, with words or without them, that in all things and at all times I seek first Thy Kingdom and Thy Righteousness. Amen.

Unum Baptisma
"One Baptism"

Part of believing in Christ and being a member of His one, holy, catholic, and apostolic Church is acknowledging one baptism for the remission of sins. Once again, a cursory glance across the spectrum of Christian denominations in the light of this affirmation might cause a certain furrowing of the brow. There are infant baptists, believers baptists, and anabaptists; there are sprinklers, pourers, and dunkers; there are those who believe in baptismal regeneration and those who insist it is only a sign; there are less frequently encountered groups such as trine immersionists (one separate and discrete dip for each Person of the Trinity, or it doesn't count) and baptizers in the name of Jesus only. And some of the more hard-line believers in these various approaches will not accept you as a real Christian unless you use their method. In some cases, it even has to be in their water. Is it really possible to discern behind these sometimes schismatic emphases the unity of one baptism for the remission of sins?

Well, let's get back to the basic facts. Christ commissioned His Church to make disciples of all nations, baptizing them in the name of the Father, the Son, and the Holy Spirit (Mat. 28:19). This practice, which sealed and made public one's decision to become Christ's disciple, had antecedents in Jewish proselyte baptism and the baptism of John the Baptist, but was identical with neither. (Those who had been baptized only with John's baptism had to be rebaptized in the name of Jesus in Acts 19:5). Baptism is a natural symbol of spiritual cleansing, and with John it was associated with repentance and confession (Mat. 3:2, 6). In Romans 6, Paul makes it a symbol of identification with Christ in His death and resurrection, hence of leaving the old life behind and beginning the new.

Unfortunately, we simply do not know whether New Testament believers baptized their children, as the Jews before them had circumcised their infant sons, or waited until they had attained an age when they could make their own profession of faith. Passages urged in favor of an answer, such as the immediate baptism of the whole household of the Philippian Jailer (Acts 16:33), are inconclusive because we simply do not know how old his children were (or even whether he had any). No passage gives explicit instruction on how the water was applied: by spargation (sprinkling), effusion (pouring), or immersion (dunking), though some are taken to imply a method. Neither does ancient tradition speak with a single voice on these questions.

I do not mean to imply that these issues are unimportant. I have my own convictions on them (believers' baptism by immersion, if you are curious). But I do believe that if they were *essential,* we would have been given clearer instructions in the New Testament itself. What is essential is that Christians be baptized in the name of the Trinity with water as a sign of their repentance from sin and a declaration of their loyalty to Christ. Baptism does not save them; it is quite clear that faith in Christ alone does that (Eph. 2:8–10). But baptism is a commanded and therefore essential expression of that faith and sign of entrance into the Christian community. Thus far all true Christians should agree. And in the absence of more clear teaching in the New Testament itself, beyond this they should agree to disagree. The central core of meaning and practice we have delineated—at least that—is the one baptism for the remission of sins that the Church acknowledges when she confesses her faith.

PRAYER: Father, the same Word without which nothing was made selected rites for His people, and should we think less wisdom and love went into that Divine choosing? Let the signs engage me as a whole person, helping me to remember that it is for the body, soul, and spirit that His redemption draweth nigh. Amen.

En Remissionem
"For the Remission ..."

We believe in one baptism for the remission of sins. This affirmation raises two questions: the nature of remission, and its relationship to baptism.

The Latin word used here means literally a sending back, hence release, letting go. When we remit a debt, we release the debtor from it, cancel it, send it back as it were marked paid in full. Remitting sins has the same effect. They are forgiven, the penalty they had merited is canceled, and God considers them as if they had never happened. He can do this because Christ died in our place on the Cross, taking the full penalty for sin on our behalf, so that those who receive Him as Savior and Lord are justified by faith.

We receive this remission through repentance and faith, which are really just two aspects of the same act. Repentance is turning from sin, and faith is turning to Christ. And these are our acts, but acts which we can perform only by grace, as the Holy Spirit enables us. For in Eph. 2:8–10, the very faith by which we receive salvation is the gift of God, worked in our hearts by His grace.

According to a good and venerable definition, a sacrament is "an outward and visible sign of an inward and spiritual grace." We would expect then that baptism would serve as an outward sign of the repentance and faith which the believer intends in the heart. And the language of Scripture confirms this.

The phrase in the Creed is a condensation of Luke's description of the baptism of John: "a baptism of repentance for the remission of sins" (Lk. 3:3). Indeed, those who came to him were baptized in the very act of confessing their sins (Mat. 3:6). Hence it seems clear that their baptism functioned as a sign of their repentance. And John goes on to distinguish his symbolic baptism with water from the reality it represents: Christ would baptize with the Holy Spirit (Lk. 3:16). It is the Spirit who actually confers the grace that allows us to repent and believe. Yet the Church continued the application of the outward symbol of this inner reality of faith and repentance, commanded to do so by the Lord Himself in the Great Commission (Mat. 28:19).

Nothing in the New Testament encourages us to believe that there is anything magical about the water or the ceremony. Those who have faith without water are saved, and those who have water without faith are lost. So how do some believers come by the notion that baptism actually confers, rather than merely symbolizing, the spiritual reality to which it points? Perhaps the short answer might be the tendency to superstition in the human heart combined with a careless reading of 1 Pet. 3:21, which seems to say that baptism saves us as the ark saved Noah. But a close reading of that verse reveals an interesting comment: "not the putting away of the filth of the flesh, but the answer of a good conscience before God." Whatever this verse means, in other words, it does not mean that baptism takes away sin. The doctrine of baptismal regeneration is denied by the very passage often urged as its prooftext.

Sins then are remitted by God's grace, on the basis of Christ's substitutionary and propitiatory sacrifice, received by faith in repentance. And baptism expresses, and by expressing, reinforces and seals or confirms that faith, thus joining us to the Community of others who share the same faith. Whether we undergo it as believers who are consciously making these commitments (as is done in my tradition) or administer it to our children in anticipation of the faith to which we pray they will come in the future, this is essentially what an Evangelical believer means when confessing one baptism for the remission of sins.

PRAYER: Father, He came to take away the sins of the world, and by grace I am enabled to say mine were among them. You leave me the memory of them to contend with the truth of their taking away. Be my defense in that warfare, Thy Word a tower of refuge. Amen.

Peccatorum
"Of Sins"

Karl Menninger once wrote a wonderful book whose title asked the provocative question, *Whatever Became of Sin?*[2] It is still a good question. As secular thinking rejects the theological grounding which once underlay the concept of the human, our ideas about humanity undergo a sea change. Once it was held to be self evident that we were *created* equal and endowed by our Creator with certain inalienable rights. Inalienable rights are tied inexorably to the doctrine of creation. For the notion of rights entails the concept of responsibility. And a free moral agent created in the image of God is a responsible person, capable therefore of having rights. But as the doctrine of creation has receded from our consciousness, we have been forced to understand ourselves by analogy with animals or machines. And they are not responsible for their behavior: it just is. We might have to destroy a dog that mauls a child, but we do not consider it evil; we do not try to reason with it. And we do not hold a trial before we put down the dog, though there might be one for its owner. Why? Because we do not consider it responsible, so we also do not accord it the same rights which we still, inconsistently, accord its master. For unless its master was in fact created in the image of God, there is no logical basis for this difference in treatment.

Because we no longer think of people as essentially different from animals, we have a hard time thinking of them as responsible for their actions. Society, or a faulty education, or bad potty training made them do it. So the doctrine of sin, of true moral guilt which accrues by virtue of evil choices for which people can rightly be held responsible and for which they can be judged, does not fit our conceptual framework very well any more. To speak of sin seems unenlightened, if not uncharitable. But have we noticed what we give up in exchange? If there is no sin because there is no responsibility, then the concept of inalienable rights becomes arbitrary and meaningless. Where do rights come from in a secular world? The government? What the government gives, the government can take away. Rights can only exist as true rights, they can only be inalienable, if they are endowed by the Creator.

But there is something even more important than our rights that we give up if we give up the doctrine of sin. And that is hope. Voltaire's Candide asks his friend Martin if he believes that "men have always massacred one another as they do today? That they have always been liars, traitors, ingrates, thieves, weaklings, sneaks, cowards, backbiters, gluttons, drunkards, misers, climbers, killers, sensualists, fanatics, hypocrites, and fools?"

Martin's reply is instructive: "Do you believe that hawks have always eaten pigeons when they could get them?"[3]

Hawks are not going to change, except by evolution, which, even if it happened, would take millions of years. And if human beings are likewise simply products of chance evolution, then for the foreseeable future we are pretty much stuck with the nature we have as well, despite Jean Luc Picard's insistence to Q that we *used* to be a savage race. But if we were created righteous and fell into sin, then we can be redeemed. That is why the seemingly insulting and negative doctrine of sin is actually full of hope. That is why our Lord Jesus Christ came down from heaven for us and for our salvation, and was made man. That is why He was crucified under Pontius Pilate and raised the third day. And that is why, when they think of their baptism in His name, Christians are reminded of the remission of sin.

PRAYER: Father, to know oneself to be found is to first have known oneself to be lost. To know oneself as seeing is to first have known oneself to be blind. Impress upon me the size of the abyss between Thee and me so that I may truly begin to understand the size of the Bridge which alone spans it. Amen.

Et Expecto
"And I Look For ..."

Because Christians believe in the remission of sins, they have hope. They have something to look forward to, to "expect," if we transliterate the Latin into English. They believe they will not be forever as they are now. In fact, they perceive that they have already begun to change. They have passed from guilt to forgiveness, from condemnation to acceptance, from alienation to adoption, from futility to purpose, indeed from death to life (Eph. 2:4–5). They can already say with e. e. cummings,

> (i who have died am alive again today,
> and this is the sun's birthday; this is the birth
> day of life and of love and wings: and of the gay
> great happening illimitably earth) ...
>
> (now the ears of my ears awake and
> now the eyes of my eyes are opened)[4]

And while they speak metaphorically thus of the present, they expect the literal fulfillment of this foretaste in the age to come. They look for the resurrection of the dead.

Hope as a theological virtue is the ability to make this forward look in such a way that the Christian vision of the future can positively affect the conduct of life in the present. It does not deny or even minimize the evils of this present world but grasps that fact that they are not the whole story. Christians see the same misery and futility as everyone else, but see them *sub specie aeternitatis,* from the perspective of eternity. There was a time when they were not; there will come a time when they will be no more. So we mourn, but not as those who have no hope. And we are able to oppose injustice and ameliorate evil in ways that would make no sense if the temporal horizon of experience were all we could see.

A positive vision of the future, in other words, makes the present different even if that future lies still a long way off. A football team that can picture itself in the Super Bowl has a much better chance of getting there than one that cannot. That vision makes a difference in the way it approaches this week's game. So powerful is this force called hope that it can sometimes create its own future. But the Christian's hope is more sure than this: it is created by the future as it exists in God's mind already. It is based, not on mere optimism or wishful thinking, but on the promises of God. Nevertheless, we do not eat mere air, promise-crammed, like Hamlet. For God has already demonstrated in the past His ability to keep such promises in the resurrection of Christ, the first fruits of those who sleep (1 Cor. 15:20). Therefore, the Christian's hope is solid nourishment indeed. For we expect the resurrection of the dead and the life of the world to come.

PRAYER: Father, instill by Thy Spirit a hope in me unshakable by mood or circumstance, a hope which makes light of the present darkness because it sees the joy set before it. Let me see the joy He saw waiting for Him on the other side of the Cross and know that joy to be the ground of my hope in Him. Amen.

Resurrectionem
"The Resurrection"

What we look for is the resurrection of the dead. Many religions believe in the immortality of the soul. But, when they are most true to the biblical vision, Christians do not have a great deal of interest in mere immortality as such. The Apostle Paul looks with distaste on the prospect of being separated from his body during the Intermediate State between death and the resurrection, but thinks it will be alright as long as he is with Christ (2 Cor. 5:1–8). And he thinks that if the dead, including Christ, rise not, we are of all men most miserable (1 Cor. 15:19).

This emphasis is present for two reasons. First, we are interested not so much in mere continued existence as in fellowship with God in Christ. Jesus Himself gave us the ultimate definition of the Christian's hope for both this life and the next: "For this is life eternal, that they might know thee, the only true God, and Jesus Christ whom thou hast sent" (Jn. 17:3). Our personal relationship with the Father through our union with Christ is not only what makes us live forever; it is also what makes it worthwhile to live that long.

Second, Christianity looks for the redemption and restoration, not just of "spirits," but of the *whole* person, including the body. Christians want to worship the spiritual God and His incarnate Son forever with both their own spirits and their bodies. The physical creation, including the body, is not, as in many religions, a barrier between human beings and the Divine. It is rather a good thing, created by God to be, not the essential but the preferred medium of the spirit. The body is not the cause of evil, but one of the things affected by sin, along with the spirit. One of the functions of humanity is to be the bridge between the worlds of matter and spirit, the unique creature who partakes of both. Thomas Browne thus calls us "that great and true amphibium, whose nature is disposed to live, not only like other creatures in divers elements, but in divided and distinguished worlds."[5] And, of course, we cannot play this role without our bodies.

This perspective may be obscured by the metaphorical use of the word "flesh" (*sarx*) in the New Testament to refer to that part of human nature not under the control of the Holy Spirit, hence fallen and evil. But that usage does not overturn our point when it is seen in context of four other facts: God's declaration that the physical creation was "good" (Gen. 1:4, 12, 18, 21, 25, 31); the fact that, while "flesh" is sometimes used with negative connotations, "body" (*soma*) is not; the incarnation of our Lord; and the doctrine of the resurrection of the body itself.

No one has ever captured the essence of our expectation of the resurrection better than Gerard Manley Hopkins:

> Like a dare-gale skylark scanted in a dull cage,
> Man's mounting spirit in its mean house, bone-
> house, dwells.
> That bird beyond the remembering its free fells,
> This in drudgery day-laboring out life's age.
> And yet on turf or perch or poor low stage,
> Each sings sometimes the sweetest, sweetest spells;
> Yet both droop deadly sometimes in their cells,
> Or wring their barriers with bursts of fear or rage.
>
> Not that the sweet fowl, song fowl needs no rest:
> Why hear him, hear him babble as he drops down
> to his nest,
> But his own nest, wild nest, no prison.
> Man's spirit will be flesh-bound when found at best,
> But uncumbered. Meadow down is not distressed
> By a rainbow footing it, nor he for his bones risen![6]

Exactly.

PRAYER: Father, what creation waits for expectantly is a redeemed humanity which will be able to say, "Touch me; I have flesh and bones." Grant that this expectation may be in my very bones themselves, lifting my chin and straightening my spine to the Kingdom's business at hand. Amen.

Mortuorum
"Of the Dead"

It is not the well who need a physician, but the sick. And it is not the living who need a resurrection, but the dead. We were warned that if we ate of the Tree from which we were commanded not to eat, in that day we would die (Gen. 2:17). And while our bodies continue to function for a while, the fact that they wear out all too soon and are subject to dissolution from the smallest bacterium, choking feather, or break in the skin shows that the threatened sentence was carried out. According to the New Testament, we are spiritually dead already, "dead in trespasses and sins" (Eph. 2:1). What does this mean?

My grandfather was an avid fisherman. He was involved in my earliest fishing trips, he had a freezer that stayed permanently packed with bass and bream, and there was always a fishing pole or two in the back of his pickup. One of the ways one could tell that he had gone on to his eternal reward was a sudden boom in the bass and bream population in the lakes of North Carolina. I don't know if there were ever any fish in the Glassy Sea that surrounds the Throne; but I know that there aren't anymore, except for the ones he has thrown back so they could grow up.

When Pa'pa died, his fishing career on earth came to a sudden end. He never went another single time. He became completely unable to pursue this activity at which he was once so skilled. But perhaps he just needs a little help. So we exhume his body and prop it up in the truck. Nothing happens. We drive the truck out to the lake, lean him against a tree, bait the hook, and put the pole into his hand. The bobber sinks, and still nothing happens. No reaction at all.

When the New Testament says that human beings apart from Christ are spiritually dead, it means that they are just as incapable of knowing, pleasing, responding to, or serving God as my grandfather is now incapable of catching fish. No amount of external assistance will help him, just as no amount of moral reformation will help those dead in their sins. The only solution is to find new life, which is precisely what is offered to us in Christ.

Sin renders us spiritually dead because it cuts us off from God, who is the only source of life. Physical death follows as a kind of sacramental sign of our rebellion, an outward and visible sign of an inward and spiritual corruption. But faith in Christ restores us to spiritual life because it makes possible, on the basis of the Atonement, a new relationship with the Father. That is why Jesus could say in Jn. 17:3 that knowing God *is* eternal life. Spiritual life resumes in Christ's followers already. They become alive to God and to all He represents, to Goodness, Truth, and Beauty, in ways that were not possible before they met Christ. Because they know God, they will live forever. And they have, as we have seen, the promise that, when Christ returns, this life will be restored in all its splendor to the wholeness of their persons, including their bodies.

To know God is to live; to be cut off from Him is to be dead. So many people that we meet, apparently alive and well, are really the walking dead. And many who have died and crumbled into dust live again already a life that began in them when they put their faith in Christ. The resurrection will translate this truth into the physical realm for all the world to see, even as it reaffirms God's commitment to whole persons, both spirit and body, as He created us. For we will all be reunited to our bodies to be adjudged either to eternal life or eternal death depending on our relationship to Christ.

PRAYER: Father, help me to see death as You see it and so see it as it is. Help me to grasp the true nature of spiritual death and to be freed from the fear of physical death so that my weeping by the beloved's grave may be as His was Who is the Resurrection and the Life. Amen.

Et Vitam
"And the Life"

We look not just for the resurrection of the dead, but the life of the world to come. The life that was already reborn in us through faith in Christ, the life that flows from Him, will be ours forever because we will be His forever. The life that sometimes now flickers faintly in the midst of the living death that sin would make of us will then be vibrant and victorious, thriving unopposed, because Christ will be all in all.

This life of the world to come is simply the life of Christ, portrayed in the Gospels, manifested in its power in the resurrection, beginning to live in us already, triumphant in His return for His own. We will share that life in reality if we have shared in His death vicariously: "I am crucified with Christ: nevertheless, I live; yet not I, But Christ liveth in me: and the life which I now live in the flesh I live by the faith of the Son of God, who loved me and gave Himself for me" (Gal. 2:20).

The connection between Christ and life in the New Testament, especially in the Gospel of John, is impressive. In Him was life (Jn. 1:4) because the Father, having life in Himself, imparts it to Him (Jn. 5:26). He came that we might have life, and that more abundantly (Jn. 10:10). He is the bread of life (Jn. 6:35), the resurrection and the life (Jn. 11:25). He is the way, the truth, and the life (Jn. 14:6). Eternal life is knowing Him (Jn. 17:3). And therefore, our life is hidden with Him in God (Col. 3:3).

Eternal life, then, is not just an endless extension of the existence we know into a boundless future. It is a mode of existence that is as much qualitatively as quantitatively extended beyond anything we can presently imagine. But *extended* is too weak a verb. Augmented, enhanced, multiplied, transformed: all these too can only hint at the abundance of life that awaits us. Knowing Him now only by faith rather than sight, seeing Him dimly, through a glass darkly, is a privilege far beyond anything we can deserve, powerful enough already to take us from spiritual death to life. But then we shall know Him as we are known, for we shall see Him face to face (1 Cor. 13:12).

Even the Twelve did not have that kind of experience except in rare glimpses, as on the Mount of Transfiguration, and they did not apparently grasp its significance very well at the time. For they knew Him, as it were, "after the flesh" (2 Cor. 5:16). And though that was a great privilege, it was not until Pentecost and the coming of the Spirit that they really understood; right up to the Ascension they were still looking for an earthly kingdom defined by the defeat of Rome (Acts 1:6).

Their new spiritual understanding coupled with their physical memories allowed them to give us the New Testament Scriptures, which, as Erasmus rightly notes, "can render [Christ] so fully present that you would see less if you gazed upon Him with your very eyes."[7] But in the world to come we will see Him with eyes fully opened in a vision transcending Scripture even as it transcends the merely fleshly understanding of the Disciples during the earthly ministry. And that will be life indeed.

PRAYER: Father, we do not yet know our future selves, but know them to be committed to His safe keeping, to be hid with Him in Thee. May my imagination be infused with the thought that what I know of life today is the shadow and copy of the Original waiting for me in Him. Amen.

Venturi Saeculi
"Of the World to Come."

We will know fully this life which is Christ in the world to come. The Latin can be translated either "world" or "age." It makes little difference, for both are true: it will be a new era indeed, for the world and time as we know them will no longer exist. Even as we ourselves become a new creation in Christ (2 Cor. 5:17), so the world also will be renewed: there will be a new heaven and a new earth (Rev. 21:1).

The world as we inhabit it now has been cursed by sin: it is "subject to futility," and hence "groans and travails" under the "bondage of corruption" (Rom. 8:18–23). The ground yields thistles and thorns instead of the wholesome fruits of Eden, a tendency which we must counteract by the sweat of our brows if we want to live. And even then, we are only fighting a rear-guard action against the ravages of Death. The best we can hope to achieve is to scatter some ruins for the archaeologists of the future to find and probably misinterpret. So much for our civilizations. And we ourselves have much ado to surpass Hamlet's cynical prophecy that a good man's memory might outlive him by half a year. The old photographs lie in the drawer, and in only a few generations it becomes hard to match the fading images with names. Others have the wherewithal to attempt more lasting monuments. But marble and the gilded monuments of princes are subject to their own foes, and around the statue of Ozymandias "the lone and level sands stretch far away."[8] A powerful rhyme, Shakespeare claims, does better. But after expending an ocean of ink, we still do not know the identity of the friend his sonnets tried to celebrate. Vanity of vanities, all is vanity, saith the Preacher.

And yet, for all this, Hopkins says, "nature is never spent."[9] And he is right. Even with the futility Sin has introduced into the fabric of nature, even with the ways we have compounded it, obscuring the beauties of the world under clouds of concrete and palls of pollution, the heavens are still able to declare the glory of God (Ps. 19:1). With the majesty of the ocean, the grandeur of the mountains, and the splendor of the night sky, the world still shouts of her Maker's greatness. The morning sun still catches the dew on a spider's web and turns it into jewels that shame anything that bedecks a monarch's crown. There is the vision of Dante, the wisdom of Spenser, the music of Milton, the language of Shakespeare. There is loneliness and loss, but there is also the clasp of a true friend's hand. And as for the way a certain lady's smile can light up a room: well.

And there is the hope of the Gospel. If this fallen world, in all its misery and futility, in spite of our inability ever to hold on to its beauties, can still speak so eloquently of its Maker, reflecting His glory and His love to the pilgrims who wander within it, then what shall we say of the world after He has restored it, healed all its wounds, and washed away all its tears? What shall we say of the world that is to come? We shall say that we "reckon that the sufferings of this present time are not worthy to be compared with the glory which shall be revealed in us" (Rom. 8:18). For we look to the life of the world to come.

PRAYER: Father, long did Thy children wait in Egypt or Babylon, despairing often, no doubt, of deliverance; yet the deliverance came. Let me occupy myself with the thought that the turning of my captivity has a precise and definite "when" to which I hasten, each day a day closer. Amen.

Amen.
"So Be it."

The word *amen* is one of the most used and least thought about of all the vocables in the English language. Its basic meaning to most people seems to be little more than, "O.K., the prayer is over now, you can open your eyes." It's actual meaning is an amalgam of the formal "So be it," the athlete's arm-pumping, celebratory "Yes!", the backwoods hot-gospeler's "Preach it, brother!", and Captain Picard's authoritative "Make it so." When we make it our final punctuation at the end of the Creed, we should be transforming a ritual reminder of the core content of our faith into a ringing affirmation of commitment.

For it is easy just to go through the motions. The motions in some churches are made week after week, and easily become routine. We may be surrounded by others for whom they have become routine. Our very leaders may encourage us to settle into an unthinking routine. I have heard celebrants who rattle the words off and hurry through them as if they were hurdles that needed to be cleared rather than signs of meaning to be pondered, of thoughts to be celebrated and embraced. The "amen" at the end is a rebuke to such approaches, a reminder to think about what we are saying and consider whether we can say it honestly.

In the preface to his wonderful little book *Who Moved the Stone?*, Frank Morison recalls that in reciting the Creed he always used to clamp his mouth shut and stay silent when he came to "and was raised the third day."[10] While it was an act of unbelief, it was also an act of integrity that placed him closer to the Kingdom than those who simply babble the same words unthinkingly. And it was that same honesty that caused him, when attempting to write a book that would refute the historical claims of the resurrection, to admit that the evidence was all on the other side. So he was converted and ended up writing the classic defense of the historicity of the resurrection of Christ. And I cannot help but believe that in his very refusal to recite the Creed without meaning—no doubt highly scandalous to his neighbors—we ironically see the early stages of our Lord's working to bring Morison unto Himself, to bring him to the point where he could open his mouth responsibly in affirming the resurrection. The thrust of the word *amen* at the end is to drive all of us along that same path.

What then is the significance of this little word at the end? These are *my* beliefs, we are saying: I own them, I claim them, I proclaim them, I celebrate them, and I stake my life on them. I stand by them. I put all my puny and inconsequential weight behind them, not because it adds anything to their credibility and worth, but because it is all I have and they deserve and demand such a response. I don't just think they are true, recognize that they are true, or even affirm that they are true, though I do all of that. I am *glad* that they are true! I worship and praise God for their truth. And I join with all my brothers and sisters of like faith around the world in making this commitment together with one voice, as the one, true, holy, and apostolic Church for which our Lord died.

And I invite you to join us in so doing.

Amen.

PRAYER: Father, the Lord Jesus is Thy "Yes" and Thy "Amen" to all Thy promises, to Thy people, to me. He is no ambiguous mix of "yea" and "nay" but a resounding trumpet blast of "Yea" to us. Let me reflect His "Amen," by loving as He loved, by keeping that faith for which He is looking when He returns. Amen.

POSTLUDE

THE NICENE CREED (SUNG)

(Can be sung to any 8.6.8.6 hymn tune, such as "Amazing Grace.")

VERSE ONE:
We believe in one true God,
    Who made both heaven and earth,
And Jesus Christ, his only Son
    By Mary given birth.
One with God before all worlds,
    Begotten, never made;
One with Man, in human flesh
    The Father's love displayed.

REFRAIN:
This Truth the Ancients left behind
    Today we still receive;
And so we worship with our minds
    And in our hearts believe.

Beneath the Roman Pilate's hand
    For us was crucified
The pure and holy Lamb of God,
    And for our sins he died.
Buried in a borrowed tomb
    Until, on the third day,
For our salvation rose again
    As Holy Scriptures say.

Exalted to the Father's side,
        From thence he shall descend
To judge the living and the dead;
        His kingdom shall not end.
And we believe the Holy Ghost
        Who glorifies the Son,
Who, with him and the Father, God
        We worship Three in One.

One holy universal church
        To serve the great I Am;
One baptism makes us all
        The people of the Lamb.
And we expect, when He returns,
        The dead to rise again.
His own will see him face to face;
        There's no more dying then.

REFRAIN:
This Truth the Ancients left behind
        Today we still receive;
And so we worship with our minds
        And in our hearts believe
That Jesus Christ is Lord of All (repeat)
        And Jesus shall be Lord of All.

D.T.W.

ENDNOTES

Part 1: The Father

1 C. S. Lewis, *The Problem of Pain* (NY: MacMillan, 1940), 19.

2 Gerard Manley Hopkins, "Pied Beauty," *The Poems of Gerard Manley Hopkins*, ed. W. H. Gardner and N. H, MacKenzie (Oxford: Oxford Univ. Press, 1962), 69.

3 Sir Thomas Browne, *Religio Medici*, 1682; *Seventeenth Century Prose and Poetry*, ed. Alexander Withrspoon and Frank J. Warnke (NY: Harcourt, Brace, Jovanovich, 1982), 339.

PART II: The Son

1 William Shakespeare, *King Lear*, act 1, scene 4.

2 *Ordo ad Representandum Herodem*, from *The Fleury Playbook*, 12th Century, *Medieval Drama*, ed. Davbid Bevington (Boston: Houghton Mifflin, 1975), 654.

3 Dante Alighiere, *Paradiso*, canto xxviii, trans. Dorothy L. Sayers (Baltimore: Penguin, 1962), 301.

4 John Milton, *Paradise Lost* I:63, *John Milton: Complete Poems and Major Prose*, ed. Merritt Y. Hughes (Indianapolis: Bobbs Merrill, 1957), 213.

5 Henry Vaughan, "The World," from *Silex Scintillans*, 1655, in Witherspoon and Warnke, op. cit., 979.

6 Dorothy L. Sayers, *The Man Born to be King* (NY: Harper and Row, 1943), 5.

7 Sir Philip Sidney, "The Defense of Poesy," 1595, *The Renaissance in England: Non-Dramatic Prose and Poetry of the Sixteenth Century*, ed. Hyder E. Rollins and Herschel Baker (Lexington, MA: D. C. Heath & Co., 1954), 607–8.

8 Dorothy L. Sayers, *The Mind of the Maker* (San Francisco: Harper & Row, 1941), esp. chp. 3.

9 C. S. Lewis, Miracles: *A Preliminary Study* (NY: MacMillan, 1947), chps. 14–16.

10 Browne, op. cit., 339.

11 C. S. Lewis, *Prince Caspian: The Return to Narnia*, 1951 (NY: Harper Collins, 1979), 233.

12 C. S. Lewis, *Mere Christianity*, 1943 (NY: MacMillan, 1960), 155.

13 Ibid., 65.

14 Gerard Manley Hopkins, "The Caged Skylark," Gardner and MacKenzie, op. cit., 71.

15 Sayers, *Man Born to be King*, op, cit., 5.

16 Lewis, Miracles, op, cit.; cf. "Myth Become Fact," *God in the Dock*, ed. Walter Hooper (Grand Rapids: Eerdmans, 1970), 63–67.

17 Milton, *Paradise Lost*, IX.782, Hughes, op. cit., 396.

18 John Donne, "Death, Be not Proud," Witherspoon & Warnke, op. cit., 757.

19 John Milton, Sonnet XIX, "When I Consider How my Light is Spent," Hughes, op. cit., 168.

20 J. R. R. Tolkien, *The Return of the King*, 1956 (NY: Ballantine, 1973), 347

21 C. S. Lewis, *Perelandra*, 1943 (NY: Simon & Schuster, 1996), 140.

22 Lewis, *Mere Christianity*, op. cit., 51.

Part III: The Spirit

1 Gerard Manley Hopkins, "As Kingfishers Catch Fire." Gardner and MacKenzie, op. cit., 90.

Part IV: The Church

1 John Milton, "Areopagetica," Hughes, op. cit., 747.

2 Karl Menninger, *Whatever Became of Sin?* (NY: Hawthorne Books, 1973).

3 Voltaire, *Candid, or Optimism, The Anthology of World Masterpieces, 5th Continental Edition*, ed. Maynard Mack et al. (NY: W. W. Norton, 1987): 1589.

4 e. e. cummings, "i thank You God for most this amazing," *Complete Poems, 1913–1962* (NY: Harcourt Brace Jovanovich, 1968), 663.

5 Browne, Religio Medici, op. cit., 339.

6 Gerard Manley Hopkins, "The Caged Skylark," Gardner and MacKenzie, op. cit., 71.

7 Desiderius Erasmus, *Enchiridion*, qtd. Marjorie O'Rourke Boyle, *Erasmus on Language and Method in Theology* (Toronto: Univ. of Toronto Press, 1982), 137.

8 Percy Bysshe Shelley, "Ozymandias," *English Romantic Poetry and Prose*, ed. Russell Noyes (NY: Oxford Univ. Press, 1956), 981.

9 Gerard Manley Hopkins, "God's Grandeur," Gardner and MacKenzie, op. cit., 66.

10 Frank Morison, *Who Moved the Stone?* 1930 (Downers Grove, IL: InerVarsityPress, n.d.), 67.

BIBLIOGRAPHY

Blaising, C. A. "Nicaea, Council of (325)." *Evangelical Dictionary of Theology*, ed. Walter A. Elwell. Grand Rapids: Baker, 1984.

Browne, Sir Thomas. *Religio Medici*, 1682. *Seventeenth Century Prose and Poetry*, ed. Alexander Witherspoon and Frank J. Warnke. NY: Harcourt Brace Jovanovich, 1982,

cummings, e. e. *Complete Poems, 1913–1962.* NY: Harcourt Brace Jovanovich, 1968.

Dante Alighiere, *The Divine Comedy*, 3 vols, 1300. Trans. Dorothy L. Sayers and Barbara Reynolds. Baltimore: Penguin, 1969.

Donne, John. "Death Be not Proud." *Seventeenth Century Prose and Poetry*, ed. Alexander Witherspoon and Frank J. Warnke. NY: Harcourt Brace Jovanovich, 1982, 757.

Erasmus, Desiderius. *Paraclesis*, qtd. in Marjorie O'Rourke Boyle, *Erasmus on Method in Language and Theology*, Toronto: Univ. of Toronto Press, 1982: 137.

Hopkins, Gerard Manley. *The Poems of Gerard Manley Hopkins*, ed. W. H. Gardner and N. H. MacKenzie. Oxford: Oxford Univ. Press, 1967.

Horton, Michael. *We Believe: Recovering the Essentials of the Apostle's Creed.* Nashville: Word, 1998.

Lewis, C. S. *Mere Christianity*. 1943. NY: MacMillan, 1960.

_________. *Miracles: A Preliminary Study*, NY: MacMillan, 1947.

_________. *Perelandra*, 1943. NY: Simon & Schuster, 1996.

________. *Prince Caspian: The Return to Narnia,* 1951. NY: Harper Collins, 1979.

________.*The Problem of Pain*. NY: MacMillan, 1941.

Menninger, Karl. *Whatever Became of Sin*? NY: Hawthorne Books, 1973.

Milton, John. John Milton: *Complete Poems and Major Prose,* ed. Merritt Y. Hughes. Indianapolis: Bobbs-Merrill, 1957.

Morison, Frank. *Who Moved the Stone*? 1930. Downers Grove, IL: InterVarsity Press, n.d.

Ordo et Representandum Herodem, from *The Fleury Playbook,* 12th century. *Medieval Drama,* ed. David Bevington. Boston: Houghton Mifflin, 1975.

Packer, J. I. and Thomas C. Oden. *One Faith: The Evangelical Consensus.* Downsers Grove, IL: InterVarsity Press, 2004.

Percival, Henry R., ed. *The Seven Ecumenical Councils of the Undivided Church: Their Canons and Dogmatic Decrees. Nicene and Post-Nicene Fathers,* 2nd Series, vol. 14, 1900. Peabody, MA: Hendrickson, 1995.

Sayers, Dorothy L. *The Man Born to Be King*. NY: Harper & Row, 1943.

________. *The Mind of the Maker*. San Francisco: Harper & Row, 1941.

Shakespeare, William. *The Complete Works,* ed. G. B. Harrison. NY: Harcourt, Brace, & World, 1968.

Shelley, Percy Bysshe, "Ozymandias." *English Romantic Poetry and Prose,* ed. Russell Noyes. NY: Oxford Univ. Press, 1956: 981.

Sidney, Sir Philip. *The Defense of Poesy,* 1595. *The Renaissance in England: Non-Dramatic Prose and Verse of the Sixteenth Century,* ed. Hyder E. Rollins and Herschel Baker. Lexington, MA: D. C. Heath & Co., 1954.

Thielicke, Helmut. *I Believe: The Christian's Creed*. Trans. John W. Doberstein & H. George Anderson. Philadelphia: Fortress, 1968.

Tolkien, J. R. R. *The Return of the King*, 1956. NY:1973. Ballantine,

Vaughan, Henry. *Silex Scintillans. Seventeenth Century Prose and Poetry*, ed. Alexander Witherspoon and Frank J. Warnke. NY: Harcourt Brace Jovanovich, 1982,

Voltaire. *Candide, or Optimism*, 1759. *The Norton Anthology of World Masterpieces*, ed. Maynard Mack, et al. NY: W. W. Norton, 1987.

Williams, Donald T. *Ninety-Five Theses for a New Reformation: A Road Map for Post-Evangelical Christianity*. Toccoa, GA: *Semper Reformanda* Publications, 2021.

________. *The Person and Work of the Holy Spirit*. Nashville: Broadman, 1994; rpt. Wipf & Stock.

________. *Stars through the Clouds: The Collected Poetry of Donald T. Williams*. Lynchburg: Lantern Hollow Press, 2020.

INDEX OF SCRIPTURE PASSAGES CITED

GENERAL INDEX

ABOUT THE AUTHOR

Donald T. Williams (BA Taylor University, M.Div. Trinity Evangelical Divinity School, PhD University of Georgia) is Professor Emeritus of Humanities at Toccoa Falls College in the hills of northeast Georgia. He is a past president of the International Society of Christian Apologetics and an ordained minister in the Evangelical Free Church of America. He has spent several summers training national pastors in places like Uganda, Kenya, and India for Church Planting International. A dual citizen of Narnia and Middle-earth, he is a border dweller, permanently camped out on the borders between serious scholarship and pastoral ministry, theology and culture, poetry and apologetics. He is the author many articles, poems, and reviews in various journals and of sixteen other books, including *The Devil's Dictionary of the Christian Faith,* 2nd edition (Middletown, R.I., Stone Tower Press, 2026).